Reza's
INDIAN
SPICE

To my parents. My father who left a great legacy
of Indian food in this country, and my mother
who has inspired me with her cooking.

Reza's
INDIAN
SPICE

EASTERN RECIPES FOR
WESTERN COOKS

REZA MAHAMMAD

PHOTOGRAPHY BY MARTIN POOLE

Quadrille
PUBLISHING

Introduction

I was born in England to Indian parents and was sent off to boarding school in India because my parents wanted me to stay in touch with their roots. So, here I am, several decades later, a product of this educational system, speaking English with a public school accent and Hindi with an English accent.

I love food. I love Indian curries, sophisticated French preparations, Thai salads, American burgers, British Sunday roasts and Persian rice dishes. Most of all, though, I love to meld them together. I live in the west, but I couldn't last a day without spices, so my solution is to tinker with classic western recipes to give them a taste of my beloved India. Indian food can be addictive. Eating a good curry releases endorphins, it's good for the soul as well as the body.

The food in this book draws from my Indian heritage, of course, but I've taken a modern, fresh approach, using ingredients which are readily available to me in England and making recipes lighter and healthier. There is classic Indian cooking, French influences from the time spent at my home in France, but also dishes taken from here, there and everywhere and given a little twist. I love to experiment with food from around the world, adding elements that bring a new dimension to a traditional recipe. No cuisine is fixed, it's always evolving, and I firmly believe in bringing a personal touch to cooking.

Spices are there to enhance food, not mask its flavours. The taste of the raw ingredients should ring loud on the palate, merely lifted and transposed to a more exciting key by the spicing. It can be delicate, aromatic, or hot, but always surprising. I prefer to use whole spices, as their flavours are fresh and intensely aromatic. You can simply grind what you need as you cook. I even make my own garam masala, which is in so many dishes; you'll find the recipe on page 24. Ready-ground spices lose potency fairly quickly. That brings me on to a note for those of you who married in the 1960s and have had the same spice rack since then. Now is the time to get rid and start all over again... they won't work! When you read the book, you'll see recipes that call for several spices. Don't be put off. Try them out even if you don't have all the ingredients. It's worth paying a visit to your local Indian shop, as you'll be able to pick up all the spices for a good price, and in one go. Once you've got them, the world is your popadum...

Second only to spice and flavour are the vibrant colours and contrasting textures which make a good dish great. I enjoy aspiring to a jewel-like opulence when I cook and, as I am sadly not dripping in rubies, pomegranates in my food will have to do!

All the dishes in this book are doable. Many are also easy: my showpiece haunch of venison, for instance, is a simple dish. You don't need special pots and pans, just a food processor or blender and coffee grinder to make the spice pastes and to save time chopping. And there are no bread recipes in this book... I'm not such a hard task master as to insist you make your own. One or two of the dishes, such as the Sweet-sour Lamb Pulao, are a little more involved, but think of it this way: if you can cook that, you can cook anything! The first time you make a recipe it will take a while, but that's only because it's unfamiliar. You'll soon become a virtuoso of the spice rack, grinding up and roasting your own concoctions with flair.

Time now to unleash your culinary skills and makes these recipes your own. I hope you have as much fun creating your own kitchen alchemy as I did conjuring up these offerings. Enjoy!

Quick *and* CHIC

Sweet potato and goat's cheese samosas

Unlike most samosas, these aren't fried. This both makes them healthier and somehow intensifies the flavour of the filling. Cinnamon is fabulous with sweet potato. I serve these with a peppery watercress dip – a kind of Indo-Italian pesto – with coriander and lemon (once, by accident, I used orange instead and it was great, so try it). If you grow nasturtiums, use the leaves instead of watercress; it tastes unbelievable. These are smart enough to serve with drinks.

1 tsp cumin seeds, plus
1–2 tbsp more, to sprinkle
400g sweet potato, diced small
salt
200g soft goat's cheese, chopped
3 spring onions, chopped
2 tbsp finely chopped coriander leaves
1 whole red chilli, deseeded if you like, finely chopped
½ tsp chilli flakes
1 tsp ground cinnamon
3 garlic cloves, crushed
125g unsalted butter
270g filo pastry
rock salt, to sprinkle

Place the 1 tsp cumin seeds in a dry frying pan and toast until golden and fragrant. Remove to a mortar and crush with a pestle. Put the sweet potato in a pan, cover with water and add salt. Bring to the boil, reduce the heat and simmer for six to eight minutes until tender. Drain and cool. Place in a bowl and mix with the cheese, spring onions, coriander, chilli, chilli flakes, crushed cumin, cinnamon and garlic. Preheat the oven to 200°C/400°F/gas mark 6.

Melt the butter. Lay a sheet of filo on a work surface and brush with butter. Place a second sheet on top to fit over the first. Brush this with butter too. Cut into strips about 5cm wide. Spoon 1 heaped tsp of filling into one corner. Fold the right corner of the strip over to the left side to create a triangle. Continue to fold the triangle along the strip to the end, cutting off surplus pastry. Repeat to use up all the pastry and filling. Brush liberally with butter and sprinkle with cumin seeds and rock salt. Bake for 12–15 minutes, until golden.

MAKES ABOUT 24

Indo-Italian pesto

30g each watercress, rocket and coriander stalks
2 garlic cloves
2 whole green chillies
70g parmesan, grated
50g pine nuts
finely grated zest of 1 unwaxed lemon and juice of 1½
200ml olive oil

Put all the ingredients except the oil into the bowl of a food processor. Start the processor, and pour the oil in slowly, until everything is smooth. Add salt to taste, and serve.

MAKES ENOUGH TO GO WITH THE SAMOSAS

Baked eggs on banana masala

I know this sounds a weird combination, but I promise you it is absolutely divine. It is a similar dish to those that the Parsis tend to eat for breakfast, but it will also make a great snack or a comforting supper. The sweetness of the bananas dances on the palate with the spicy onions and sharp tomatoes... try it, I dare you!

6 ripe bananas, peeled and sliced into 5mm rounds
juice of ½ lime or lemon
3 tbsp vegetable oil or ghee
3 onions, finely sliced
½ tsp turmeric
2 garlic cloves, crushed
2.5cm piece of root ginger, grated
2 green chillies, deseeded if you like, finely chopped
½–1 tsp chilli powder, to taste
1 tbsp tomato purée
2 large tomatoes, finely chopped
1 tsp ground cinnamon
salt
½ tsp caster sugar
3 tbsp chopped coriander leaves
6 eggs
1 tsp freshly ground black pepper, or chilli flakes

Place the bananas in a bowl and sprinkle with the lime or lemon juice to prevent them discolouring. Set aside.

Heat the oil into a wide, heavy-based pan over a medium-high heat until hot. Add the onions, turmeric, garlic and ginger and cook until the onions turn a light golden brown. Reduce the heat and add the chillies, chilli powder and tomato purée. Stir-fry for a minute, then add the tomatoes, cinnamon, salt to taste and sugar. Cook until the sauce is well reduced and not watery. Now add the coriander and bananas. Mix gently but thoroughly and remove from the heat. Preheat the oven to 190°C/375°F/gas mark 5.

Spread the mixture evenly into a baking dish, then make six hollows in it with the back of a spoon. Break each egg into a hollow. Sprinkle some salt and pepper or chilli flakes over the eggs.

Cover with aluminium foil and bake for 10–15 minutes, or until the eggs are done to your liking.

SERVES 3 ON ITS OWN, OR 6 AS PART OF A SPREAD

Spicy crab cakes

A great alternative to western-style fish cakes, which can sometimes be bland, these have a far greater depth of flavour. Crab meat is enhanced beautifully by both mustard and fennel seeds, in fact the intensity of crab is actually softened by the spices here.

FOR THE CRAB CAKES
150g potatoes
3–4 tbsp vegetable oil,
plus more to deep-fry
2 tsp black mustard seeds
1 tsp fennel seeds
8 curry leaves, shredded
1 onion, finely chopped
½ tsp turmeric
2 tsp grated root ginger
2 tsp crushed garlic
2 finely chopped green chillies
1 tsp chilli powder
600g white crab meat
juice and finely grated zest
of 1 lime
2 tbsp chopped chives, or
2 spring onions, chopped
1 tbsp chopped coriander leaves
salt
freshly ground black pepper

TO COAT
100g plain flour
2 eggs, lightly beaten
250g toasted dried breadcrumbs

Boil the potatoes in their skins until tender to the point of a knife. Drain them and, when cool enough to handle, slip off their skins and grate them coarsely.

Heat the oil in a wide pan over a medium heat until hot, then add the mustard and fennel seeds. Once they begin to crackle, add the curry leaves, onion and turmeric. Cook until the onion becomes soft and translucent. Now add the ginger, garlic and chillies. Sauté for a minute or so, then add the chilli powder. Stir-fry for a few more seconds, then add the crab. Stir-fry until all the moisture has been absorbed. Fold in the potato and remove from the heat. Add the lime juice and zest and the herbs, season to taste, then allow to cool.

Put the flour, eggs and breadcrumbs into three separate bowls. Shape the crab meat into eight patties. Lightly dust each in flour, then dip into the egg, and finally coat with the breadcrumbs.

Heat the oil for deep-frying in a deep pan or wok until it reaches 175°C/345°F. Add the patties in batches, being careful not to crowd the pan, and deep-fry for about two minutes, turning once, until golden brown all over. Remove with a slotted spoon and drain on kitchen paper. Serve while still piping hot.

SERVES 4

Serve with **Sambal with Lemon Grass** *(see page 139), or* **Tomato and Ginger Chutney** *(see page 22)*

Marinated smoked salmon with yogurt, herbs and spices

You have to try this, it's fab. It is not at all difficult, but will be a new technique for many people. It is called *dhungar*. A piece of smouldering charcoal is sealed in a tray with the salmon, so the smoke is captured in the marinade. It's a great way of imbuing smokiness if you don't have a barbecue, and you may well find you start cooking this way with lots of other things, as it's just amazing... the flavour reverberates at the back of the palate. Make sure that the salmon is pin-boned (you can ask the fishmonger to do this for you). You will need a large piece of charcoal to smoke the fish and some bamboo skewers.

FOR THE MARINADE
3–4 tbsp yogurt, lightly whisked
1 tsp turmeric
1 tsp chilli powder
3 tbsp wholegrain mustard
3 garlic cloves, crushed
2cm piece of root ginger, grated
3 tbsp runny honey
1–2 green chillies, deseeded if you like, finely chopped
finely grated zest of 1 unwaxed lemon and juice of ½
2 tbsp finely chopped coriander leaves
2 tbsp finely chopped dill
2 tbsp finely chopped chives
salt

FOR THE SALMON
600g salmon fillets, pin-boned and cut into 5cm chunks
6 green cardamom pods
4–6 cloves
1 tbsp ghee

In a mixing bowl, combine all the ingredients for the marinade and rub well on to the salmon pieces. Leave to marinate for 30 minutes.

Arrange the salmon pieces in a single layer in a roasting tin, making a space in the centre.

Using metal tongs, heat a piece of charcoal over a gas flame on the hob until it is red hot, then transfer to a small metal bowl. Place the bowl in the centre of the roasting tin. Sprinkle the cardamom and cloves straight on to the charcoal, then pour the ghee over it. As soon as it starts to smoke, cover the tin tightly with foil to trap the smoke. Allow to marinate further for a few hours in the refrigerator.

When you are ready to cook, bring the salmon to room temperature while you preheat the oven to 190°C/375°F/gas mark 5. Soak some bamboo skewers in warm water for 30 minutes.

Thread the salmon pieces on to the skewers. Suspend the fish from the skewers over a roasting tin, so none of the fish touches the tin, and put into the oven for six to eight minutes, basting the salmon with any of the leftover marinade. Remove from the oven and allow the salmon to rest on a cooling rack for a couple of minutes before removing the skewers.

SERVES 4

Serve with Cucumber Raita *(see page 139), and* Beansprout Salad with Chargrilled Asparagus and Coconut *(see page 116)*

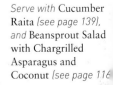

Roasted red mullet with spicy tomato salsa

Once, when I was in France, I ate an amazing fish à la grenobloise, with lemon segments and capers. I thought it would be so nice to spice the recipe up, but not too much because red mullet is a delicate fish. You could use grapefruit segments instead of lemon here, if you prefer; there's nothing better than wedges of citrus with a fresh tomato salsa. The lovely sweet-sharp-sour quality from the chaat masala in the salsa is delicious with the red mullet, giving it an amazing *je ne sais quoi*! Serve with rice or glass noodles if you want something else. Fabulous!

FOR THE SPICE MIX
½ tsp coriander seeds
½ tsp fennel seeds
½ tsp black peppercorns
1 tsp red chilli flakes

FOR THE MULLET
4 red mullet fillets, each weighing 160g, scaled and pin-boned
salt
4–6 garlic cloves, thinly sliced
100ml vegetable or mild olive oil

FOR THE SALSA
250g ripe tomatoes, deseeded and sliced
100g red onions, thinly sliced
3 unwaxed lemons, zest finely grated and fruit segmented
80ml olive oil
1 tsp chaat masala
1–2 thin green chillies, deseeded if you like, finely chopped
4–6 sprigs of coriander, leaves picked and chopped
caster sugar, to taste

Mix together the coriander and fennel seeds and the peppercorns and roast them in a dry frying pan. Crush them coarsely in a mortar and pestle and add the chilli flakes. Rub the mixture on to the fish fillets and set aside for 20 minutes.

Preheat the oven to 160°C/325°F/gas mark 3.

Place the fillets on a baking tray and season with salt, add the garlic and drizzle over the oil. Cook for about 10 minutes.

Meanwhile, combine all the ingredients for the salsa in a mixing bowl, adding salt and sugar to taste.

Remove the fish from the oven and place on warmed plates. Pour any of the juices from the fish into the salsa. Spoon the salsa over the fish and serve.

SERVES 4

Fish in coriander chutney

A traditional Parsi dish, this is so delicious and everyone loves it, with the vibrant green herbs and sweet coconut. The Parsis were persecuted in Iran during the 10th century and fled to India, bringing their style of cooking with them. This dish has a beautiful tangy taste which comes alive when it is steamed in its parcel in the oven. You can use any type of white fish. It is steam-baked so keeps lovely and moist. Banana leaves are widely available in Thai and Indian grocers and they impart a beautiful flavour, but if you can't find them, foil or baking parchment make fine substitutes.

4 x 150–180g thick, firm white fish fillets (try cod loin, whiting, sea bass, pomfret or hake)
salt
6 green chillies, deseeded, plus 2 whole green chillies
100g freshly grated coconut, or 75g desiccated coconut
1 very large bunch of coriander leaves and stalks, roughly chopped
30–40g roughly chopped mint leaves
1 tsp cumin seeds
8 garlic cloves
2–3 tsp caster sugar
2 tbsp lime or lemon juice
banana leaves or foil, to wrap the fish
a little vegetable oil (optional)

Briefly rinse the fish, then pat dry with kitchen paper and salt lightly.

Using a food processor or blender, grind together the chillies, coconut, coriander, mint, cumin seeds, garlic, sugar and lime juice into a thick paste, adding a small amount of water if required. Adjust the seasoning. Coat each fish fillet with the paste on both sides. Preheat the oven to 190°C/375°F/gas mark 5.

Remove the stems from the banana leaves, if using, and cut into squares each large enough to wrap a fillet. Secure gently by tying with string, or with the stems from the leaves. Or use foil, oiling it lightly to stop the fish from sticking.

Place the fish on a metal rack in a baking tray and pour in enough water to cover the base of the tray, making sure the level of the water does not reach the rack. Place in the hot oven and steam-bake for 20–25 minutes, or until the fish flakes to the point of a knife.

Remove the strings or stems from the parcels. Serve the fillets in their parcels, allowing your diners to open them at the table to release the delicious aromas. Serve with yogurt flavoured with lemon zest, a squeeze of lemon juice, salt, pepper and a little sugar.

SERVES 4

Serve with **Khichri** *(see page 129)*

Chilli-seared mackerel

There are times when nothing hits the spot quite like fried fish, served with khichri (lentils and rice) and dollops of yogurt. This is Indian comfort food, which for me conjures up memories of holidays at my grandparents' home on the western Ghats. This recipe works equally well given a European twist, with Beetroot and Radish Salad (see page 114). I love the spicy fish contrasted with the sweet, earthy flavours of roasted beets and the peppery crunch of radish. I've been using a lot of rapeseed oil lately; it's a good one for searing as it has a high smoke point.

FOR THE MARINADE
4 garlic cloves, grated
1 tbsp grated root ginger
1 tsp chilli powder
1 tsp turmeric
2 tbsp lime juice
salt

FOR THE MACKEREL
850g mackerel fillets
rapeseed or vegetable oil, to shallow-fry
lime wedges, to serve

FOR THE CHILLI PASTE
8 green chillies, deseeded, plus
3 whole green chillies
2 tsp ground coriander
2 tsp ground cumin

Mix all the ingredients for the marinade in a small mixing bowl. Place the mackerel fillets in a large, shallow dish and coat them evenly with the marinade mixture. Cover with cling film and refrigerate for 30 minutes.

Meanwhile, prepare the chilli paste. In a small blender, process together the chillies, coriander, cumin and a pinch of salt with a small quantity of water to a very smooth paste.

After 30 minutes, remove the fish from the fridge and evenly coat the fillets with the chilli paste.

Heat the oil in a large, wide frying pan over a medium-high heat. Fry the fish, skin side down, for three minutes (it is best to do this in batches of three). Turn the fish and continue to fry for a further three minutes. Remove from the pan and drain on kitchen paper. Serve, piping hot, with lime wedges for squeezing.

SERVES 4

Serve with Beetroot and Radish Salad *(see page 114), or* Khichri *(see page 129)*

Lemon and coriander chicken

There's not much to this very simple dish, but it is divine and far more than the sum of its parts. The chicken is enhanced by the taste of the ginger and garlic and just a hint of chilli. A lovely, comforting dish for winter, you'll find this soon becomes a go-to recipe. Top tip: if you put a lemon in the microwave for 10 seconds, you will be able to squeeze out the maximum amount of juice.

150g yogurt
finely grated zest and juice of
1 unwaxed lemon
2 onions, finely chopped
4–6 tbsp vegetable oil or ghee
½ tsp turmeric
5 garlic cloves, crushed
2 tsp grated root ginger
1 tsp chilli powder
salt
900g chicken breasts, skinned and cut into 3cm cubes
3 green chillies, deseeded if you like, finely chopped
4–6 tbsp finely chopped coriander leaves

Lightly whisk the yogurt with half the lemon zest and set aside.

Fry the onions in the oil or ghee until they turn a deep almondy colour. Add the turmeric, garlic, ginger, chilli powder and some salt. Stir-fry these spices together for a few seconds or so, then add the chicken. Continue to stir, frying the chicken and spices together for a few minutes until they are well combined and the chicken turns a pale golden brown. Add the yogurt mixture a little at a time to the pot. Keep stirring until thoroughly incorporated with the spices.

Reduce the heat, cover and simmer for eight to 10 minutes. Now add the green chillies, coriander and the lemon juice with the remaining zest. Stir well and simmer for 10–15 minutes, or until tender.

SERVES 4–6

Serve with **Perfect Rice** *(see page 132), or* **Spinach with Radish Greens** *(see page 129)*

Spicy chicken burgers

We are used to seeing chicken burgers sold cheaply on every high street, but don't worry... this burger's in a league of its own! Minced chicken can be boring, but the mushrooms in this burger mix makes it stay lovely and juicy and the spices send it to a heavenly level. Serve the burgers in toasted buns, with sliced onion and tomato, lettuce leaves and chutney.

1 heaped tsp cumin seeds
100g mushrooms
500g minced chicken
1 onion, grated
2 tsp grated root ginger
2 tsp crushed garlic
1–2 green chillies, deseeded if you like, finely chopped
3 tbsp chopped coriander leaves
finely grated zest of 1 lime
2 tsp garam masala
salt
freshly ground black pepper
vegetable oil

Put the cumin seeds into a dry frying pan over a medium heat and stir until they are fragrant and have turned a shade darker. Tip into a mortar and grind to a powder with the pestle.

Blitz the mushrooms in a food processor. Put all the ingredients except the oil into a mixing bowl, knead well and combine thoroughly. Cover and refrigerate for 30 minutes or so. Divide into eight portions and form each into a burger shape.

To cook, you can shallow-fry the burgers over a medium heat in a frying pan or on a griddle. For a healthier option, lightly brush the burgers with oil and place on a rack under a hot grill. Turn halfway through cooking. In either case, the burgers should only take three minutes each side. Check they are thoroughly cooked: cut a burger through to the middle, it should be white with no trace of pink.

SERVES 4

Tomato and ginger chutney

A great relish for your burger, this is a wonderful all-rounder. It would be lovely with Crab Samosas (see page 76), or Spiced Vegetable Polenta (see page 121).

3 tbsp vegetable oil
½ tsp asafoetida
½ tsp chilli powder
5 tbsp chopped root ginger
250g tomatoes, diced
1 tbsp tomato purée
200g jaggery or brown sugar
2 tsp mustard seeds
20 fresh curry leaves
5 dried red chillies, halved

Heat 2 tbsp of the oil in a pan and, when hot, add the asafoetida and chilli powder. Allow to sizzle, then add the ginger and cook for two minutes. Add the tomatoes and tomato purée and cook until the tomatoes begin to break down. Add the jaggery and 120ml of water and cook on a low heat for 10 minutes, or until the mixture thickens.

Put the remaining oil into a frying pan over a high heat. When very hot, add the mustard seeds, curry leaves and dried chillies. Add to the chutney. Stir and add salt to taste.

SERVES 4–6

Chicken tikka with fenugreek

A Punjabi-style dish from the land of the five rivers, this dish shows off the indulgent, verdant flavours of the state. Punjab is famous for tandoori dishes, and the food also displays the wonderful influences from neighbouring Iran, Afghanistan and central Asia. The rich, herby flavours of the landscape ring through with the distinct earthiness of fenugreek. The morsels of meat are really moist, with an extraordinary, complex taste.

TO MAKE GARAM MASALA
8 bay leaves
6–8 x 5cm cinnamon sticks
50g coriander seeds
50g cumin seeds
1 tbsp fennel seeds
1 tbsp black peppercorns
1 tbsp cloves
2 tbsp green cardamom pods
4–6 black cardamom pods
4–6 star anise
8–10 blades of mace
1–2 tbsp dried rose petals

FOR THE CHICKEN
600g skinless chicken breast, cut into 5cm cubes
2 tbsp melted butter or ghee

FOR THE FIRST MARINADE
8 garlic cloves, grated
1 tbsp grated root ginger
juice of ½ lemon
salt

FOR THE SECOND MARINADE
1½ tsp cumin seeds
200g fresh fenugreek leaves
4 green chillies
3 tbsp dried fenugreek leaves
4 tbsp mustard oil
1 tbsp vegetable oil
250g Greek yogurt
1 tbsp gram flour
1 tsp garam masala

I can't recommend enough that you make your own garam masala for Indian dishes; sure you can buy it everywhere, but this knocks the socks off any pre-ground tub. To make it, dry-roast all the ingredients in a wide, non-stick pan for five to seven minutes, stirring. Grind in a coffee or spice grinder to a very fine powder. Store it in an airtight container in a cool, dark place and use it up as soon as you can.

Now to the chicken. Put it in a mixing bowl and add the ingredients for the first marinade. Cover and refrigerate for 30 minutes to one hour. Meanwhile, put the cumin seeds for the second marinade into a small dry frying pan, place over a medium heat and stir until aromatic and a shade darker. Pour into a mortar and crush to a powder with the pestle.

Bring a saucepan of water to the boil, add the fresh fenugreek leaves and blanch for a few minutes until the leaves turn soft. Drain in a colander, then put into a food processor or blender. Add the chillies, dried fenugreek leaves and roasted cumin. Blend to a smooth paste. In a frying pan, heat both the oils and cook the fenugreek paste for about five minutes, stirring continuously. Remove from the heat, put into a bowl and allow to cool. Fold in the yogurt, gram flour and garam masala, and adjust the seasoning.

Remove the marinated chicken from the fridge. Fold in the fenugreek marinade. Return the chicken to the fridge and allow to marinate for at least four hours, or overnight. Bring the chicken pieces to room temperature, then place on a grill tray. Grill under a hot grill for about four minutes on each side, basting with the melted butter or ghee halfway through cooking. Serve with any of the salads or chutneys in this book, or with a raita.

SERVES 4

Serve with Shredded Green Mango Pickle *(see page 139)*

Beef satay

Serve this with a vibrant salad for a lovely contrast of colours and textures; the rich, spicy satay works well with a burst of freshness next to it. You can use chicken or pork fillet instead of beef, if you prefer. If you don't have a chargrill pan, the skewers can be cooked for the same amount of time under a hot grill, or on a barbecue. You can buy frozen kaffir lime leaves from any Thai grocery, they defrost in seconds.

FOR THE BEEF
400g fillet of beef, or sirloin, or tenderloin
12–16 bamboo skewers
a little vegetable oil

FOR THE PASTE
4 tbsp unsalted peanuts
1 tbsp coriander seeds
1 tsp cumin seeds
4 tbsp chopped red shallots
1 tsp turmeric
4 kaffir lime leaves, very finely chopped
2.5cm piece of root ginger, finely chopped

FOR THE SAUCE
250ml thick coconut milk
2 tbsp condensed milk
2 tbsp palm or soft brown sugar
2 tbsp fish sauce
pinch of salt

Cut the beef into strips of about 5 x 2cm, against the grain. Place in a bowl and set aside.

To make the paste, put the peanuts in a dry frying pan over a medium heat and cook, stirring, until toasted. Tip them into a blender or food processor. Place the coriander and cumin seeds in the frying pan and dry-fry them, too, until toasted. Put them into a mortar and grind to a powder with the pestle. Add to the peanuts with all the other paste ingredients. Blitz to a very smooth paste, adding just enough water to help it along. Decant into a bowl.

Combine all the ingredients for the sauce in a separate bowl, then add half of it to the peanut mixture and stir well. Add the beef and mix, allowing the meat to absorb the marinade. Cover, refrigerate and allow to marinate for four to six hours or, ideally, overnight.

When ready to cook, soak the bamboo skewers in a bowl of warm water for 30 minutes, so they don't catch fire when you cook them, and return the beef to room temperature.

Thread three pieces of meat on to each skewer and push down tightly. Place a lightly oiled chargrill pan over a high heat. When hot, cook the skewers for two minutes on each side, basting with some of the remaining sauce. Serve the rest of the sauce as a dip.

SERVES 3–4

Serve with Mooli and Pomegranate Salad *(see page 112)*

Spicy beef salad

A dish which captures the vibrant, aromatic freshness of the East, this speaks for itself and needs no other accompaniment. A lovely light lunch, this will also serve two as a more substantial meal, or you could use a little more steak if you want to stretch it to serve four.

FOR THE SALAD
2 tbsp dark soy sauce
1 tbsp soft dark brown sugar
370g rump steaks
1 cucumber, peeled, deseeded and thinly sliced
1 tomato, deseeded and thinly sliced
6 radishes, thinly sliced
½ red onion, thinly sliced
1 tbsp chopped coriander leaves
1 tbsp vegetable oil
50g pomegranate seeds (optional but lovely)

FOR THE DRESSING
2 tbsp Thai sweet chilli sauce
juice of 2 limes and finely grated zest of 1
1 garlic clove, crushed
1 red chilli, finely sliced
2 tsp fish sauce
1 sprig of mint, leaves shredded

Mix together the soy sauce and brown sugar and pour on to the steak. Leave to marinate for 30 minutes.

In the meantime, mix together all the ingredients for the dressing and set aside.

In a separate bowl, mix together all the vegetables and herbs for the salad and set aside.

Heat the vegetable oil in a frying pan until hot but not smoking. Shake off any excess marinade from the steaks and sear them for two to three minutes on each side. They will be rare to medium-rare. Remove and leave to rest for 10 minutes.

Cut the beef into thin slices and place in a bowl. Add a few spoons of the dressing and toss. Fold in all the salad ingredients, sprinkle with pomegranate seeds, if using, and fold in a little more dressing, serving the rest on the side at the table.

SERVES 2–3

Lassis

Lassis are always served with meals in India, from breakfast to supper. They are used as a coolant in the hot weather. Think of lassis as yogurt-based smoothies. All the lassis here, both sweet and savoury, are perfect with hot food. About one litre of lassi will serve four people.

Mint and cumin

1 tsp cumin seeds
650g Greek yogurt
about 2–3 tbsp chopped mint leaves, plus more leaves to serve
½ tsp freshly ground black pepper
finely grated zest of 1 lime and juice of ½
1 tbsp caster sugar
ice cubes
salt, to taste

Pour the cumin seeds into a small, dry frying pan and place over a medium heat. Stir until aromatic and a shade darker, then tip into a mortar and grind to a powder with the pestle.

Put the crushed cumin seeds into a jug blender and shove in all the remaining ingredients with a big handful of ice cubes and about 1 tsp of salt, or to taste.

Blitz until smooth. Pour into chilled glasses and sprinkle with mint leaves to serve.

MAKES ABOUT 1 LITRE

Roasted fig

12 fresh figs, ideally Black Mission
juice of ½ lemon
4 tbsp runny honey
½ tsp ground cardamom
2 tsp sumac
500g Greek yogurt
100ml whole milk
ice cubes

Preheat the oven to 180°C/350°F/gas mark 4.

Cut the figs into quarters and drizzle over the lemon juice and honey. Sprinkle over the cardamom and half the sumac. Roast in the hot oven for 10–15 minutes. Remove and allow to cool.

Put the yogurt, milk and cooled figs with their juices into a blender or smoothie maker with a few ice cubes. Blitz until smooth. Pour into chilled glasses and sprinkle with the remaining sumac to serve.

MAKES ABOUT 1 LITRE

Rhubarb

600g rhubarb
125g caster sugar
5cm piece of root ginger, grated
finely grated zest and juice of
1 orange
ice cubes
500g Greek yogurt

Peel the rhubarb and de-string if needed. Cut into chunks. Place in a saucepan with the sugar and ginger. Cook until tender (it will take about 10 minutes). Remove from the heat and allow to cool. Add the orange zest and juice.

Reserving a few spoonfuls, place most of the rhubarb compote in a blender or smoothie maker, with a few ice cubes and the yogurt.

Blitz until smooth. Serve topped with the reserved rhubarb compote.

MAKES JUST OVER 1 LITRE

Minted mango

12 ice cubes, plus more to serve
850g can mangoes in syrup
500g natural yogurt
8 mint leaves
pinch of ground cardamom
2 tbsp caster sugar
juice of ½ lemon

Add the ice to a jug blender with the remaining ingredients, reserving a little of the mango to serve. Blend until smooth.

Add a few more ice cubes to a glass and pour over the lassi. Serve with the reserved mango, chopped, on top.

MAKES JUST UNDER 1.5 LITRES

Strawberry and cardamon

300g strawberries
4–6 tbsp caster sugar
1 tsp ground cardamom
½ tsp black peppercorns,
crushed
1½ tsp rose water
400g Greek yogurt
ice cubes

Hull and chop the berries. Add sugar to taste, the cardamom, pepper and rose water. Leave for 30 minutes for the strawberries to release their juices.

Purée the strawberries in a blender. Remove a few spoonfuls and set aside. Add the yogurt to the blender with a few ice cubes and blitz until smooth. Serve with the reserved strawberry purée on top.

MAKES 800ML

Slow
BURNERS

Panchrattan (five jewels) dal

A darling of dals. The combination of these five different lentils, each with their own texture and taste, is a traditional Rajasthani idea. This is my interpretation of the dish. It is very rich and full of flavour, nourishing, healthy and earthy, so serve it simply with rice or a chapati. You may find it too thick – it is supposed to be so – but add a little water if you prefer a thinner dal. Asafoetida is known as 'devil's dung' because of its potent aroma, and it is added to dishes containing beans and lentils as it is an anti-flatulent. Fresh curry leaves come in big bags, and freeze very well; just defrost them for a few minutes, pat them dry with kitchen paper and chuck them in the pan.

FOR THE DAL

20g urad dal (white lentils)
50g mung dal (green lentils)
20g toor dal (oily/waxy lentils)
20g chana dal (yellow lentils)
25g masoor dal (red lentils)
1 tsp turmeric
a little asafoetida
salt
3 tbsp ghee or vegetable oil
1 heaped tsp cumin seeds
1 large onion, thinly sliced
6 garlic cloves, thinly sliced
3–4 green chillies, slit
1½ tbsp julienned root ginger
leaves from 2 sprigs of fresh curry leaves
½ tsp garam masala
juice of 1 lime
1–2 tbsp chopped coriander leaves

TO SERVE

2 tbsp ghee or vegetable oil
1 tsp chilli powder
dollop of yogurt

Wash all the lentils in warm water until the water runs clear. Soak in warm water for about one hour, then drain.

Put the drained lentils into a heavy-based saucepan with 800ml water. Bring to the boil and remove any scum that forms. Now add the turmeric and a generous pinch of asafoetida. Cover and simmer until the lentils are almost cooked, then add some salt. Allow the lentils to cook until tender, but still retaining their textures.

Heat the ghee or oil until hot in a wide frying pan, then add another pinch of asafoetida and the cumin seeds. Once they begin to splutter, add the onion and fry until it starts to brown at the edges. Now add the garlic, chillies and ginger. Continue to fry until the whole mixture turns golden brown, then toss in the curry leaves.

Meanwhile, heat the 2 tbsp ghee or oil to serve until hot, then add the chilli powder. Once hot, pour over the yogurt in a small bowl.

Toss the onion mixture on to the lentils with the garam masala. Stir in the lime juice and the chopped coriander. Serve in bowls with the yogurt on the side.

SERVES 4

Serve with
Perfect Rice
(see page 132)

Spicy stuffed potatoes

A real meat-eating boy's dish, this is hearty comfort food. It's delicate yet rich and based on a Persian dish. It's almost like an upside-down eastern shepherd's pie... though, of course, a glorified version. There's nothing better than mince and potatoes together. This is an economical meal to make if you are on a budget, and a new way to use minced meat.

4 large potatoes of similar size
4 tbsp vegetable oil, plus more to fry the potatoes
2 large onions, thinly sliced
1 tsp crushed garlic
225g minced lamb
2 tbsp tomato purée
1 tsp ground cinnamon
1 tsp ground allspice
2 tbsp chopped coriander leaves
1 tbsp chopped mint leaves
2 tbsp chopped flat leaf parsley leaves
2 eggs, hard-boiled and chopped
salt
freshly ground black pepper
300ml tomato juice
200ml beef stock
½ tsp caster sugar

Wash and peel the potatoes. Cut a small slice from the bases to stop them wobbling around, then remove a 'lid' from the top and set aside. Hollow out the potatoes with a melon baller, creating a shell about 1cm thick. Discard the potato pulp.

Heat some oil in a frying pan until hot and brown the potatoes and their lids. Remove with a slotted spoon and drain on kichen paper.

In a separate pan, heat the 4 tbsp of oil until hot and add the onions. Sauté until the onions are soft, then add the garlic and continue to cook for a minute. Now add the minced lamb and cook until the meat is browned all over. Stir in the tomato purée along with half the cinnamon and allspice. Mix thoroughly and continue to cook for several minutes. Now add the herbs, eggs, salt and pepper and mix thoroughly. Remove the pan from the heat and allow to cool slightly. Preheat the oven to 180°C/350°F/gas mark 4.

Fill the potatoes with the stuffing, replace the tops, then arrange the potatoes in an ovenproof dish.

Mix together the tomato juice, stock, remaining cinnamon and allspice, the sugar and seasoning to taste. Pour the mixture around the potatoes, cover and bake in the oven for about an hour, or until tender, basting occasionally with the juices. Adjust the seasoning and serve with flat bread, fresh herbs and Persian pickles.

SERVES 4

Serve with
Kachumbar
(see page 114)

Sweet and sour stuffed chicken

This magnificent roast bird shows the influence of Middle Eastern cuisine, which I love, and makes a fantastic alternative to a plain roast dinner. In fact, it started out as a Middle Eastern recipe, before I stuck my oar in and Indianised it. The fruity stuffing is just fabulous, with the sweet dried apricots and raisins playing against the hot ginger and chilli; it also keeps the chicken moist, basting it from within while it roasts.

FOR THE CHICKEN
1 x 1.5kg chicken
salt
freshly ground black pepper
100g ghee or vegetable oil

FOR THE MARINADE
finely grated zest and juice of 2 oranges
finely grated zest and juice of 1 lime
2 tsp chilli flakes
1½ tsp ground cinnamon
1½ tsp ground allspice
3–4 garlic cloves, grated
1 tbsp root ginger, grated

FOR THE STUFFING
1 large onion, thinly sliced
2 garlic cloves, crushed
2.5cm piece of root ginger, grated
175g pitted prunes, soaked and finely chopped
175g dried apricots, soaked and finely chopped
1 apple, peeled, cored and chopped
40g raisins
50g pine nuts, toasted
1 tsp ground cinnamon
½ tsp ground allspice
1 tsp chilli flakes
2 tbsp chopped coriander leaves

Rinse the chicken and pat dry with kichen paper. Rub with salt and pepper and place in a baking dish large enough to hold it.

Combine all the ingredients for the marinade in a mixing bowl and pour over the chicken. Wearing kitchen gloves, carefully ease the skin of the chicken from the flesh over the breast and legs, starting from the head end. It is very important that the skin remains intact, so do proceed with caution and try not to break it! Gently spread some of the marinade mixture under the skin. Allow to marinate in the fridge for at least three hours, or preferably overnight, spooning the marinade over the chicken occasionally.

In a frying pan, heat 2 tbsp of the ghee or oil over a medium heat. Add the onion and garlic and fry until the onion turns a golden brown. Now add the ginger and stir for a further minute. Add everything else except the coriander and gently sauté for another five minutes. Finally add the coriander and allow the mixture to cool.

Preheat the oven to 190°C/375°F/gas mark 5.

Remove the chicken from the baking dish, retaining all the marinade in the dish. Stuff the chicken with the fruit mixture and truss. Return the chicken to the baking dish, spoon over the marinade and brush with the remaining ghee or oil. Cover loosely with foil. Place in the hot oven and roast for 1½ hours, basting occasionally and removing the foil after 40 minutes to allow the skin to brown and crisp. Allow to rest, tented with foil, for 20 minutes, then carve and serve.

SERVES 6

Serve with **Roast Potatoes with Chilli and Chaat Masala** *(see page 115), and* **French Beans with Sesame Seeds** *(see page 118)*

Persian chicken with saffron and cardamon

Royal chickens destined for Indian palace tables were massaged with musk oil and sandalwood and fed on pellets infused with saffron and rose water, so the flavours permeated the flesh of the birds. Our more humble chickens – lacking the spa treatment – haven't had that kind of life, but the rule that what goes in must come out still applies, so do buy the best bird you can afford. I have included black cumin in this recipe. If you can't find any, just use normal cumin. Black cumin is also known as *shahi jeera*, similar looking to caraway seeds, and thinner, darker and slightly sweeter than normal cumin. It really does enhance this dish, so if you happen to come across it, snap it up. It is so important when you fry onions – and especially in this dish – that you don't hurry them. Fry them until properly sweet and gilded and don't go too quickly; we're not looking for scorched, still-raw, 'hot dog' onions! It can take more time than you'd think but, to get ahead, organised people can fry a big batch, drain them until very dry indeed and store in an airtight container, to add to all sorts of dishes. They will keep for up to a week.

4–6 tbsp ghee or vegetable oil
4 large onions, finely sliced
1.7kg chicken, skinned and jointed into 8
6–8 garlic cloves, crushed
1 tbsp grated root ginger
1 tsp chilli powder
½ tsp ground black cumin
1½ tsp freshly ground black pepper
250g yogurt
120ml single cream
salt
seeds from 12–15 green cardamom pods, ground
1 tsp saffron threads
juice of ½ lime
1 tbsp chopped coriander leaves
1 tbsp toasted flaked almonds

Heat the ghee or oil in a wide, heavy-based pan and fry the onions until they turn a deep golden brown. Remove the onions with a slotted spoon and drain on kitchen paper. When cool, blend them coarsely in a food processor. Set aside.

Fry the chicken pieces in the same fat over a medium-high heat to seal in the juices. Reduce the heat slightly and add the garlic and ginger. Fry for a minute, then add the chilli powder, black cumin and pepper, and sauté well. Lightly whisk the yogurt, cream and salt to taste with half the ground cardamom and pour over the chicken. Cover and simmer on a low heat for 20–25 minutes, until tender.

In the meantime, lightly toast the saffron threads over a low heat, then crumble them over the blended fried onions along with the remaining cardamom. Stir this mixture into the chicken and simmer for a further minute or so. Finish off with the lime juice, coriander and almonds.

SERVES 4

Serve with
Kidney Beans with Dried Lime
(see page 124)

Royal leg of lamb

A simplified version of a palace dish – *shahi raan* – and beautifully rich and impressive. *Shahi* means royal and this has certainly been given the royal treatment. Check the sauce when you baste the lamb: if it looks dry, add water. For pink lamb, only cook for two hours in total.

FOR THE LAMB
1.5kg leg of lamb
5 tbsp ghee or vegetable oil, plus more for the tray
1 tbsp flaked almonds, toasted
2 tbsp chopped mint leaves

FOR THE FIRST MARINADE
1½ tbsp white poppy seeds
2 tbsp flaked almonds, plus more to serve
1–2 tbsp raisins
2 tbsp cashew nuts
2 onions, cut into chunks
6 garlic cloves, roughly chopped
6cm piece of root ginger, chopped
6 green chillies
6 tbsp chopped coriander leaves and stalks, plus more to serve
juice of 1 lemon
salt

FOR THE SECOND MARINADE
3 onions, thinly sliced
300g Greek yogurt
½ tsp saffron threads, steeped in 3 tbsp hot milk for 10 minutes

FOR THE SPICE MIX
3 star anise
3–4 blades of mace
2–3 cassia barks or cinnamon sticks
8–10 green cardamom pods
3 black cardamom pods
1½ tsp black peppercorns
2–3 bay leaves
1 tsp fennel seeds

Trim off the parchment-like skin and surface fat from the lamb, or get your butcher to do it. Slash it all over and place in an oiled roasting tray. For the first marinade, in a frying pan, toast the poppy seeds until they exude a nutty aroma and become a few shades darker. Put into a bowl with the almonds, raisins and cashews. Pour over 80–100ml of boiling water and soak for 15 minutes. In the same pan, dry-fry the onion chunks until they soften and form brown patches. Add to the nut mixture. Put the nut and onion mixture, with the soaking liquid, into a blender with the garlic, ginger, chillies, coriander, lemon juice and salt. Blend to a fine paste. If the paste is too coarse, add a little water. Massage the mixture over the lamb and into the slashes. Cover and refrigerate for two to three hours.

Heat 3 tbsp of the ghee in a frying pan over a medium heat and add the sliced onions. Fry until golden brown. Remove with a slotted spoon and drain on kitchen paper, reserving the ghee. Put two-thirds of the onions into a blender with the yogurt and saffron milk. Blend to a fine paste. Put all the spices for the spice mix into a frying pan and gently toast until they release their wonderful aromas. Remove from the heat and grind to a fine powder in a coffee or spice grinder. Mix 2–3 tsp of the spices into the yogurt mixture and season with salt (store the rest in an airtight container for up to six weeks; you'll definitely use it again!). Allow to infuse for an hour. Remove the lamb from the fridge and massage in the yogurt mixture. Return to the fridge and marinate overnight.

Preheat the oven to 200°C/400°F/gas mark 6. Return the lamb to room temperature. Pour over the ghee from the onions, the remaining 2 tbsp ghee and 300ml water. Cover with foil and cook for 30 minutes, basting once. Reduce the oven temperature to 170°C/340°F/gas mark 3½ and cook for about three hours, basting every 30 minutes, until the meat falls off the bone, adding a further 300ml water halfway through. If the sauce starts to dry out too fast, keep adding water and continue to baste.

Serve on a platter garnished with toasted flaked almonds, the reserved fried onions and chopped mint.

SERVES 6

Serve with Jewelled Rice *(see page 135), or* Saffron Rice *(see page 134)*

Lamb with ginger

A lovely aromatic, warming dish for the very cold days of winter. There is no garlic in this at all, just ginger and other aromatic spices. It is a very simple recipe in which the flavours of the lamb are merely enhanced by the gentle, fragrant spicing.

1 tbsp grated root ginger
500g Greek yogurt
750g lean lamb, in 5cm cubes
3 tbsp ghee or vegetable oil
4–6 cloves
2 x 5cm cinnamon sticks
1 black cardamom pod, bruised
4 green cardamom pods, bruised
salt
1 tsp ground ginger
1 tsp chilli powder
1 tsp freshly ground black pepper
¼ tsp grated nutmeg
¼ tsp ground mace
1 tsp garam masala
1 tbsp chopped coriander leaves

Combine the ginger and yogurt in a bowl and add the meat. Mix well and leave to marinate for about one hour.

Heat the ghee or oil in a heavy-based pan and add the cloves, cinnamon and both types of cardamom pods. Fry for a few seconds, then add all the marinated meat. Bring to the boil and cook, stirring continuously, until most of the liquid dries up.

Add salt to taste, the ground ginger, chilli powder, black pepper, nutmeg and mace. Stir well and cook for five minutes. Add 500ml of hot water, cover and simmer until most of the liquid is absorbed and the meat is tender (about 45 minutes). Add the garam masala and cook for a further five minutes. Remove the cinnamon sticks and cardamom pods. Finally sprinkle with the coriander and serve.

SERVES 4

Serve with **Spinach and Leek Rice** *(see page 133)*

Lamb dopiaza

'Dopiaza' simply means 'double onions'. In this dish, the onions are added in two different ways: one is a ground raw onion paste; the other the fried variety. Onions have long been considered an aphrodisiac. You may be titillated to know that, in the 15th century Arabic sex manual, *The Perfumed Garden*, Abu-el Heiloukh ate onions and remained stimulated for 30 uninterrupted days. Read into that what you will, but perhaps this is not a dish for the faint hearted.

2 onions, roughly chopped, plus 3 onions, finely sliced
4 garlic cloves
5cm piece of root ginger, roughly chopped
3 green chillies
6 tbsp ghee or vegetable oil
6 cloves
8 cardamom pods, crushed
2 tsp cumin seeds
1 tsp crushed peppercorns
2 sprigs of fresh curry leaves
800g lamb, in 5cm cubes
¼ tsp turmeric
1 tsp ground cumin
1 tsp ground coriander
200g yogurt, lightly whisked
2 tsp garam masala
salt
2 tbsp chopped coriander leaves

In a food processor, blend together the chopped onions, the garlic, ginger and chillies into a smooth paste, adding a dash of water to help break them down. Decant into a bowl and set aside.

In a heavy-based pan, heat the ghee or oil over a medium-high heat, then fry the sliced onions until golden brown. Remove with a slotted spoon and drain on kitchen paper, reserving the oil in the pan.

Put the reserved oil back on the heat, then add the cloves, cardamom, cumin seeds, peppercorns and curry leaves. Allow the spices to crackle for a few seconds, then add the onion paste. Reduce the heat slightly and stir-fry for five to seven minutes, making sure it does not brown.

Increase the heat, then add the meat. Brown it all over, then add the turmeric, ground cumin and coriander. Continue to stir-fry for a few minutes. If the mixture begins to stick, add a dash of water and continue to stir-fry. Now add the fried onions, reserving a small handful to serve. Continue to stir-fry for a further two to three minutes, then fold in the yogurt with 1 tsp of the garam masala. Mix thoroughly and continue cooking, stirring all the time. Now add 250ml of hot water, bring to the boil, reduce the heat, cover and simmer for about 45 minutes, or until the meat is tender.

Add the remaining garam masala and adjust the seasoning. Scatter with the chopped coriander and reserved fried onions and serve.

SERVES 4

Serve with
Perfect Rice
(see page 132)

Braised and fried beef

A wonderful dish, rich, dark and reminiscent of a Malaysian rendang, this is one of those recipes where the pot does most of the cooking for you. Don't be daunted by the long ingredients list, all of the spices are familiar and many are doubled up to make the same flavours in the first and second stages. This recipe is fantastic with chapatis, parathas, pitta or Middle Eastern lavash bread. The cooking method is vital here: once the beef has been braised until tender, the liquid is removed and then the meat fried until really dark and rich.

FOR THE SPICE MIX
3 dried red chillies
2 tsp coriander seeds
1 cinnamon stick, broken in half
½ tsp black peppercorns
3 cloves
1 tsp turmeric

FOR THE BEEF
750g stewing steak, cubed
2 onions, sliced
3cm piece of root ginger, shredded
3 fat garlic cloves, finely chopped
2 sprigs of curry leaves
3 green chillies, deseeded if you like, shredded
50ml vegetable oil

FOR THE FRYING STAGE
4–5 tbsp vegetable or corn oil
4 shallots, sliced
3 garlic cloves, sliced
1 red pepper, sliced
1–2 sprigs of curry leaves
2 green chillies, deseeded if you like, finely chopped
2 tsp ground cinnamon
2 tbsp chopped coriander leaves

First, make the spice mix. Put the dried red chillies, coriander seeds, cinnamon stick, peppercorns and cloves in an coffee or spice grinder and process to a fine powder. (Or pound the spices in a mortar and pestle.) Stir in the turmeric.

Put the beef in a large, heavy-based saucepan and add the onions, ginger, garlic, curry leaves, chillies and oil. Mix well. Add the spice mix, barely cover the meat with water, then put on the lid and simmer on a low heat for about two hours, until the beef is tender. Add more water during the cooking process if it is drying out. Now drain off any remaining liquid into a bowl and set aside.

Now for the frying stage: heat the oil in a frying pan and add the beef and any reserved cooking liquid. Fry the meat until it turns a really rich dark brown. Now add the shallots, garlic, red pepper, curry leaves, chillies and cinnamon. Allow all the vegetables to soften for five minutes or so. Finish by stirring through the chopped coriander. Serve immediately.

SERVES 4

Serve with **Sambal with Lemon Grass** *(see page 139) and* **Coconut Rice** *(see page 132)*

Spiced meatballs in tomato sauce

A great wintry comfort dish that is lovely either with mashed potatoes or with plain rice. As you may have gathered by now, I adore Middle Eastern food, and this recipe has wonderful Indo-Middle Eastern tones. It is especially useful to have in your repertoire on those days when you only have minced meat in the fridge, but are desperate to make something new and exciting with it! Serve it with a cooling raita, if that takes your fancy.

FOR THE MEATBALLS
750g lean minced lamb, ideally from the leg
1 heaped tbsp finely chopped mint leaves
2 heaped tbsp finely chopped coriander leaves
2 garlic cloves, crushed
4cm piece of root ginger, grated
2 green chillies, deseeded if you like, chopped, or 1 tsp cayenne pepper or chilli powder
1½ tsp ground cumin
1 heaped tsp ground cinnamon
salt
freshly ground black pepper

FOR THE SAUCE
3–4 tbsp vegetable oil
1 largish onion, finely chopped
2 garlic cloves, crushed
1 tsp ground cumin
½ tsp chilli powder or flakes
250ml lamb stock
690g bottle tomato passata
caster sugar, to taste

TO SERVE
a dollop of yogurt
2 tsp roughly chopped mint leaves
1 tbsp roughly chopped coriander leaves

First, put all the ingredients for the meatballs into a bowl, season very well and mix thoroughly. (This mixture can be covered and left to marinate in the fridge for 30 minutes or overnight, if it's easier.) When ready to cook, roll the mixture into walnut-sized balls.

Heat the oil for the sauce in a wide saucepan, add the onion and garlic and cook over a medium heat until the onions completely soften. Add the cumin and chilli powder or flakes and sauté for a couple of minutes. If the mixture begins to stick, add a splash of stock and continue to cook for a further minute. Now add the remaining stock and reduce by two-thirds. Add the passata, sugar and salt, to taste. Bring to the boil and, once the sauce begins to bubble, add the meatballs. Return to the boil, reduce the heat, and simmer for 30–40 minutes, until the meatballs are tender.

Remove to a serving dish and garnish with a dollop of yogurt and the roughly chopped herbs.

SERVES 4

Serve with **Perfect Rice** *(see page 132)*, *or* **Saffron Rice** *(see page 134)*

Sweet-sour lamb pulao

One of the oldest recorded types of pulao, with a wonderful combination of sweet and sharp. It's the most complicated rice dish in this book, but all the elements can be made ahead, making the day itself simply an assembly job.

FOR THE MEAT

500g shoulder of lamb, cubed
1 tsp coriander seeds
½ tsp cumin seeds
1 onion
2 black cardamom pods, crushed
1 tsp ground black peppercorns
1 tsp ground cinnamon
½ tsp crushed anise seeds
4–6 cloves, coarsely ground
½ tsp ground mace
2 bay leaves
1 tsp crushed garlic
1 tsp grated root ginger

FOR THE RICE

350g basmati rice
½ tsp saffron threads
6–7 tbsp ghee or rapeseed oil
4 onions, thinly sliced
100g caster sugar
juice of 3 limes
1½ tsp chilli powder
3 tbsp flaked almonds, toasted
3 tbsp slivered pistachios
3 tbsp raisins
3 tbsp toasted coconut
100ml meat stock
100ml whole milk
2 tbsp orange flower water

FOR THE SAUCE

3–4 tbsp ghee or rapeseed oil
1 tbsp grated root ginger
2 tsp chilli powder
120g yogurt
2 tsp ground coriander
1 tsp garam masala

Put the meat in a saucepan, cover with water, add a pinch of salt and bring to the boil. Skim, and simmer for five minutes. Drain the meat and rinse. Place the coriander and cumin seeds in a dry frying pan over a medium heat. Stir until they smell aromatic, then grind to a powder. Roughly chop the onion, then place in a blender and process to a paste. Return the meat to the rinsed-out saucepan and cover with fresh water, adding all the other ingredients. Bring to the boil and simmer for 45 minutes, or until tender. Remove the meat with a slotted spoon. Strain the liquid through a sieve, then pour into a clean pan and reduce until you have about 240ml left.

Wash the rice in warm water then rinse in cold. Soak for 30 minutes in salted water. Soak the saffron in 2 tbsp hot water. Bring 1.5 litres of water to the boil in a pan, add salt and 2–3 tbsp ghee. Rinse and drain the rice and add to the water. Boil for five minutes, until the rice pops to the surface. Drain and pour cold water over to prevent further cooking. Now to the sauce. In a non-stick heavy-based pan, heat the ghee, then add the meat, some salt, the ginger, chilli and yogurt. Fry until browned. Add the ground coriander and garam masala and sauté for two minutes. If it sticks, add a dash of water.

Preheat the oven to 220°C/425°F/gas mark 7. Fry the sliced onions in a little more ghee until golden, drain, then set aside. Mix the sugar, lime juice and chilli powder. Mix the nuts, raisins and coconut and the stock, milk and orange flower water in two separate bowls. You now have five components aside from the rice: the lime solution; fruit and nuts; fried onions; stock; saffron. Get them all to hand.

Grease a heavy-based pan with ghee. Spread in one-quarter of the rice and sprinkle with some saffron, a small handful of both nuts and onions and some of the lime. Spread more rice on top, then add the meat. Put the remaining rice in a bowl and mix in the remaining lime and most of the remaining nuts and onions, reserving a little of both. Spread this over the meat and drizzle with the remaining saffron and ghee. Pour on the stock. Cover and bake for 20 minutes, reduce the temperature to 180°C/350°F/gas mark 4 and bake for 40 minutes. Serve on a platter, sprinkled with the reserved nuts and onions.

SERVES UP TO 4

Serve with Smoked Aubergine Raita with Sesame Seeds *(see page 138)*

Showing
OFF

Stuffed chillies

This makes a fabulously impressive starter. A note for the chilli weaklings: this is definitely a dish worth trying, because the large chillies are not at all hot; they have almost the taste of a sweet pepper, with a very rich filling.

FOR THE CHILLIES
8–10 large chillies

FOR THE STUFFING
2–3 tbsp vegetable oil,
plus more to deep-fry
1 tsp black mustard seeds
1 tsp cumin seeds
1 red onion, finely chopped
¼ tsp turmeric
½ heaped tsp grated root ginger
½ heaped tsp crushed garlic
2 green chillies, finely chopped
180g cooked potatoes, chopped
80g paneer, grated
2 eggs, hard-boiled, chopped
salt
1–2 tbsp finely chopped
coriander leaves
juice of 1 lime
1 tbsp toasted sesame seeds

FOR THE BATTER
80g gram flour
1 tsp ajwain (carom) seeds,
(optional)
½ tsp chilli powder
2 tsp amchur (mango powder,
optional)
½ tsp turmeric

FOR THE DIP
1 onion, roughly chopped
80g chopped coriander leaves
2 garlic cloves
1 green chilli
juice of ½ lemon
5 tbsp yogurt
1 tbsp tahini
1 tsp caster sugar

Slit each large chilli down the middle and carefully remove and discard all the seeds and membrane.

Heat the 2–3 tbsp oil in a wide frying pan until it just begins to smoke, then tip in the mustard and cumin seeds. Once they pop and crackle, add the onion and turmeric. Cook until the onion turns soft, then add the ginger and garlic. Sauté for a minute or so, then add the chillies and potatoes. Stir-fry for a minute or two, then add the paneer. Cook for a further minute, then add the eggs with some salt. Stir fry for another 30 seconds. Remove from the heat, stir in the coriander, lime juice and sesame seeds and adjust the seasoning. Leave to cool.

Put all the ingredients for the batter in a bowl with 200ml of chilled water and mix well.

Once the stuffing has cooled down, use it to stuff the chillies and set aside. Blitz together all the ingredients for the dip in a food processor or blender, until smooth.

Heat the oil for deep-frying in a large wok or kadhai on a medium heat. Once the oil becomes hot, dip the chillies into the batter then drop into the hot oil. Deep-fry until crisp and golden, turning to brown them on all sides. Drain on kitchen paper and serve, piping hot, with the dip.

SERVES 4 AS A STARTER

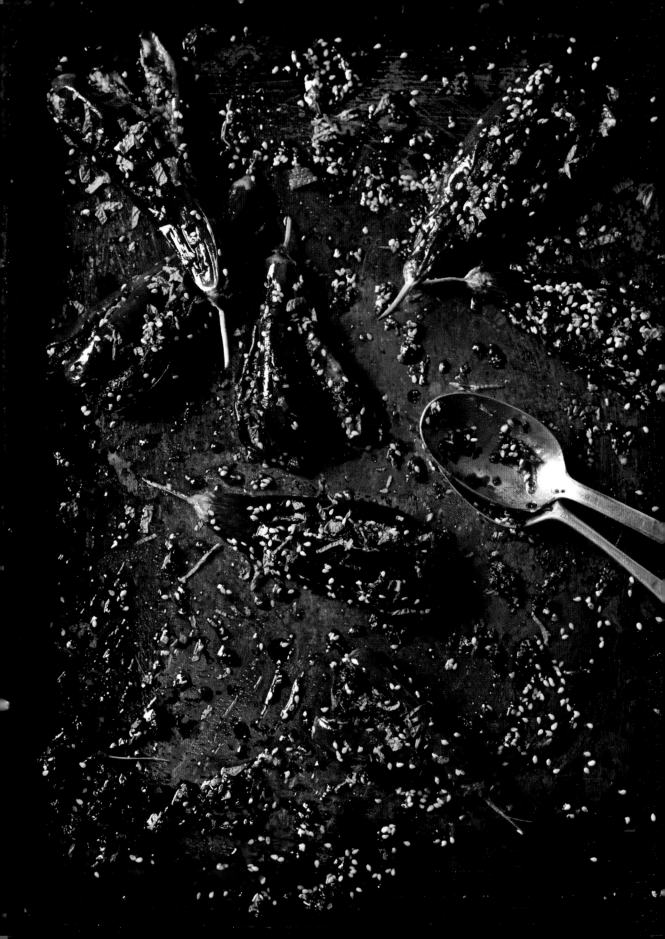

Baked baby aubergines

My mother made the most amazing baked aubergines and I have tried to recreate this dish of my childhood. The sweetness of the lime solution works beautifully, but you must make sure that the sugar completely dissolves in the lime. The stuffing can be made a day or two before, and the dish assembled and baked on the day. All the juices are absorbed by the aubergines and it will play havoc with your tastebuds... in a lovely way, of course.

12 baby aubergines (about 450g)
salt
¼ tsp turmeric
4–6 tbsp ghee or vegetable oil
6–8 onions, thinly sliced
10 cloves
2 x 5cm cinnamon sticks
2 black cardamom pods
6–8 green cardamom pods
1½ tsp black peppercorns
1 tsp ground allspice
3 tsp chilli powder
5cm piece of root ginger, grated
60g caster sugar
juice of 2–3 limes
generous handful of finely chopped mint leaves
1 tbsp toasted sesame seeds

Preheat the oven to 180°C/350°F/gas mark 4.

Make two deep slits in each aubergine, forming a cross from the base towards the stalk end, but leaving the quarters attached at the stalk to hold the aubergines together. Rub the aubergines with some salt and the turmeric. Set aside for 30 minutes.

Meanwhile, heat the ghee or oil in a wok or a large, deep frying pan and fry the onions to a golden brown. Remove and drain on kitchen paper, reserving the ghee or oil.

In a coffee or spice grinder, grind together half the cloves, and the cinnamon sticks, black and green cardamom pods and peppercorns to a fine powder. Add the allspice and mix well. Set aside.

When the onions are cool and crispy, process two-thirds of them to a paste in a food processor, remove and put into a bowl. Reserve the other third. To the onion paste, add 2 tsp of the chilli powder, the ginger and the ground spices and combine well. Stuff the aubergines with the onion paste mixture and place in a baking dish.

Heat the reserved ghee or oil in a pan and add the remaining whole cloves. Once they darken, remove and discard the cloves and pour the flavoured ghee over the aubergines. Cover with foil and bake in the oven until fully tender; it should take 40–45 minutes.

Meanwhile, mix the sugar, lime juice and remaining chilli powder in a small saucepan, heating gently until the sugar dissolves, forming a syrupy solution. Drizzle over the aubergines, then return to the oven for a further five minutes. Drain off any excess ghee or oil and sprinkle with the reserved onions, chopped mint and sesame seeds.

SERVES 4–6 AS A SIDE DISH

Serve with Panchrattan Dal *(see page 34),*
or Broad Beans with Yogurt, Garlic and Dill *(see page 83)*

Stuffed, spiced courgettes

Stuffed vegetables are common in Indian cookery, but the raisins and toasted pine nuts here add a Mediterranean twist. Courgettes act as 'stunt doubles' for the more exotic and hard-to-find gourds we would stuff. I use cottage cheese here because it's more easily available than paneer, but if you can find or make good paneer, use that instead.

FOR THE COURGETTES

4 large courgettes, each weighing 150g
a little rapeseed or vegetable oil

FOR THE FILLING

2 tbsp rapeseed or vegetable oil
1 tsp cumin seeds
1 tsp fennel seeds
1 shallot, finely chopped
1 tsp crushed garlic
1 tsp grated root ginger
2 green chillies, finely chopped
2 tbsp raisins
2 tbsp finely chopped coriander leaves
2 tbsp finely chopped chives
200g cottage cheese
30–40g pine nuts, toasted

FOR THE SAUCE

2 onions, roughly chopped
4 tbsp rapeseed or vegetable oil
1 tbsp crushed garlic
1 tbsp grated root ginger
700g tomatoes, liquidised
3 tbsp tomato purée dissolved in 1 tbsp water
1 tsp chilli powder
1 tsp ground cumin seeds
1 tsp ground fennel seeds
¼ tsp tumeric
1 tsp caster sugar
salt

Cut the courgettes in half lengthways and scoop out the seeds with a teaspoon to form a deep hollow. Finely chop the scooped-out flesh and set aside.

In a frying pan, heat the oil. Add the cumin and fennel seeds. Allow to pop and splutter, then add the shallot, garlic, ginger and chillies. Cook until the chopped shallot has softened and become translucent. Add the scooped-out courgette flesh and sauté until all the moisture has evaporated (about six to eight minutes). Remove from the heat and add the raisins. Allow the mixture to cool.

Add the coriander, chives, cottage cheese and pine nuts. Stuff the courgettes. Preheat the oven to 180°C/350°F/gas mark 4.

To make the sauce, blend the onions in a blender with 200ml of water to a smooth paste. Heat the oil in a wide, heavy-based pan over a medium-high heat until hot. Add the onion paste, garlic and ginger. Cook until it turns a light brown. (Do not worry if the onions absorb all the oil, just keep cooking until the mixture changes colour.) Add the tomatoes, tomato purée, chilli powder, ground cumin, ground fennel and turmeric and continue to cook for a few minutes. Add the sugar and adjust the seasoning with salt.

Pour the mixture into a roasting tray. Place the stuffed courgettes on top and drizzle with oil. Cover with foil and bake in the hot oven for 35–40 minutes, until the courgettes are tender.

Serve with yogurt seasoned with ground roasted cumin seeds.

SERVES 4

Serve with **Spinach with Radish Greens** *(see page 129)*

Paupiettes of lemon sole with saffron sauce

This dish epitomises my love for 'Frindian' food, combining classic French methods with an Indian twist! It not only looks elegant and refined, with the white fish contrasting beautifully with the yellow sauce, but the taste is subtle yet complex. It is a perfect recipe to impress, without hours spent in the kitchen. Don't be alarmed by the list of ingredients, the preparation is straightforward. If you want to add extra oomph, serve with potato straws (see page 67) for a bit of crunch.

FOR THE FILLING

300g raw prawns (shelled, deveined weight)
1 tsp grated root ginger
2 tbsp finely chopped chives
1 tbsp finely chopped dill
1 tbsp finely chopped coriander leaves
finely grated zest of 1 unwaxed lemon and juice of ½
¼ tsp roughly crushed fennel seeds
¼ tsp chilli flakes
salt

FOR THE SOLE

6 x 140–160g fillets of lemon sole, trimmed and skinned
freshly ground black pepper
150ml dry white wine or vermouth
a little vegetable oil

FOR THE SAUCE

2 tbsp rapeseed or vegetable oil
1 tsp fennel seeds
2 shallots, finely chopped
2 garlic cloves, crushed
1 tsp grated root ginger
1 green chilli, finely chopped
½ tsp saffron threads
1 tbsp chopped coriander leaves
200ml double cream

Preheat the oven to 180°C/350°F/gas mark 4.

First, make the filling. Blitz the prawns coarsely in a food processor. Decant into a bowl and mix in all the remaining ingredients, with salt to taste. Divide into six portions and set aside.

Place the sole fillets, skinned side up, on a work surface. Lightly season with salt and pepper. Place a portion of the prawn stuffing on each of the fillets. Roll the fillets, starting with the thickest part and finishing with the tail. Place in a roasting tray and pour over the wine or vermouth. Cover with an oiled sheet of baking parchment and place in the hot oven for 10–12 minutes, until cooked through.

Meanwhile, make the sauce. Heat the oil in a pan until hot, then add the fennel seeds and allow them to pop for a few seconds. Add the shallots, garlic, ginger and chilli, reduce the heat to medium and cook until the shallots are soft and transparent.

Once the fish is cooked, remove from the oven and pour the juices from the roasting tray into the sauce. Cover the fish and keep warm.

Add the saffron and coriander to the sauce, then reduce the liquid by half, so the flavours intensify. Add the cream and cook for a couple of minutes until the sauce has thickened, become glossy and coats the back of a spoon. Strain through a sieve, pushing through the juices to maximise the flavours, then adjust the seasoning.

With a sharp knife, cut each paupiette in half, allowing three halves per portion. Arrange on a plate and pour the sauce around.

SERVES 4

Serve with Gingered Carrots with Maple Syrup *(see page 125)*

Scallops with coconut and ginger

An easy dish which takes just minutes. The sauce here is very south Indian in inspiration, based on a moilee. You could use it with prawns as well, to delicious effect. The delicate flavours of the scallops are enhanced by the lovely, velvety, creamy sauce and not overwhelmed by spice; actually, the spices bring out flavours from the shellfish and give it a lift.

FOR THE SCALLOPS
1 tsp coriander seeds
½ tsp cumin seeds
1 tsp chilli flakes
500g king scallops
1 tbsp vegetable oil
1 tsp sea salt

FOR THE SAUCE
2 tbsp coconut or vegetable oil
10 curry leaves
1 onion, sliced
2.5cm piece of root ginger, grated
4 green chillies, slit lengthways
½ tsp turmeric
500ml coconut milk
1 tsp salt
25g caster sugar

Place the coriander and cumin seeds in a dry frying pan and toast until golden and wonderfully fragrant. Remove to a mortar and crush them with a pestle. Set aside.

Now make the sauce. Heat the oil in a large frying pan, add the curry leaves, onion, ginger and green chillies. Cook and stir until the onion is soft, then add the turmeric, followed by the coconut milk, salt and sugar. Bring to a simmer and cook for three to five minutes, until the sauce begins to turn glossy and thickens enough to coat the back of the spoon. Keep warm.

Mix together the ground, toasted coriander and cumin seeds and the chilli flakes and coat the scallops to give an even crust. Heat the oil until hot in a large frying pan, then add the scallops. Sear for about one minute on each side until golden, sprinkle salt on each and remove from the pan. Serve with the warm sauce. These would be lovely served on top of a mound of spinach.

SERVES 4

Serve with
Coconut Rice
(see page 132), and
Spinach with Radish
Greens *(see page129)*

Spice-crusted monkfish in tomato sauce

A great showing off dish and very simple. Both sauce and spice crust can be made in advance. The two marinades are there for a reason: the first for spiciness, the second to add moisture. The lemon grass gives an almost Thai flavour to the sauce. You could serve this with mashed or boiled potatoes and it would work beautifully.

FOR THE SPICE MIX
1 tsp coriander seeds
1 tsp cumin seeds
1 tsp black peppercorns
1 tsp fennel seeds
1 dried red chilli

FOR THE FISH
800g monkfish
1 tbsp vegetable or rapeseed oil

FOR THE FIRST MARINADE
1 tsp grated root ginger
½ tsp crushed garlic
½ tsp ground black pepper
juice of ½ lemon
salt

FOR THE SECOND MARINADE
1 tbsp grated cheddar cheese
2 tbsp Greek yogurt
1 tbsp grated root ginger
2 green chillies, finely chopped
1 tbsp chopped coriander
1 tbsp double cream

FOR THE TOMATO SAUCE
8 ripe tomatoes, chopped
4 tbsp ghee or rapeseed oil
1 bay leaf
1 tsp grated root ginger
1 tsp crushed garlic
1 tsp ground cumin
1 tsp ground fennel
1 tsp chilli powder
3 lemon grass stalks, crushed
300ml coconut milk

First make the spice mix. Put all the ingredients in a small frying pan and lightly toast over a low heat, until they turn a shade darker and release their aromas. Coarsely grind in a mortar and pestle.

Place the fish in a flat roasting tray. Mix together all the ingredients for the first marinade. Rub over the fish and cover with cling film. Refrigerate for 30 minutes.

Mix together all the ingredients for the second marinade in a small mixing bowl, folding in the cream at the end. Cover and refrigerate

Now to make the sauce. Blitz the tomatoes with a small amount of water in a blender to a smooth paste. Pass through a fine sieve to remove any seeds. Heat the oil in a sauté pan over a medium-high heat. Add the bay leaf, ginger and garlic and fry for a minute or so, then add the tomatoes, the cumin, fennel, chilli powder and lemon grass. Bring to the boil, then simmer for five to eight minutes. Stir occasionally to prevent the sauce from sticking. Now add the coconut milk and continue to simmer until the sauce becomes glossy, then adjust for salt and cook for a minute or so. Preheat the oven to 200°C/400°F/gas mark 6.

Remove the fish and the bowl of the second marinade from the fridge and bring to room temperature. Pour the second marinade over the fish and sprinkle the spice mix on top. Place in the hot oven and cook for 10 to 12 minutes, or until the fish begins to flake. Reheat the tomato sauce over a medium heat and discard the lemon grass. Place the fish on a serving dish and drizzle the sauce around.

SERVES 4

Serve with **Spinach with Radish Greens** *(see page 129), and* **Perfect Rice** *(see page 132)*

Guinea fowl, herb butter and wild mushrooms

In my most humble opinion, guinea fowl has far more flavour than chicken. It is the perfect type of bird to cook in the autumn or winter months, as it is fuller and more substantial in flavour than chicken. All the recipes in this book for marinated chicken pieces would also work well with guinea fowl, so ring the changes every now and then. The influences of this dish are French, so this is yet another of my 'Frindian' dishes. It's lovely with creamy mashed potato.

FOR THE HERB BUTTER
125g unsalted butter, softened
3–4 garlic cloves, crushed
finely grated zest of 2 unwaxed
lemons and juice of 1
2 tbsp finely chopped
tarragon leaves
1 tbsp finely chopped
coriander leaves
1 green chilli, finely chopped
1 tsp pink peppercorns, crushed
salt

FOR THE GUINEA FOWL
2 guinea fowls, jointed (total
weight about 1.5kg)

FOR THE MUSHROOMS
1 tbsp mild olive or vegetable oil
2 garlic cloves, crushed
1 shallot, finely chopped
300g assorted wild mushrooms
juice of ½ lemon
1 tbsp chopped tarragon leaves
1 tbsp chopped chives
½ tbsp chopped
coriander leaves

Combine all the ingredients for the herb butter in a mixing bowl, with salt to taste, then chill in the refrigerator for 20 minutes. Preheat the oven to 200°C/400°F/gas mark 6. Spread a generous amount of the butter under the skin of each of the guinea fowl joints. Smear any leftover herb butter over the skin and sprinkle with some salt. Place in a roasting tin and roast in the hot oven for 40–45 minutes, or until the juices run clear when you push a knife into the thickest joint, basting twice during the cooking process.

Remove from the oven and allow to rest for 10 minutes, covered with foil. Remove the excess fat from the pan juices.

Meanwhile, heat the oil over a medium-low heat and add the garlic. Cook for a few seconds without burning, then add the shallot. Sauté until the shallot becomes soft and transparent. Add the mushrooms and stir-fry until they have shrunk, then add the lemon juice and the guinea fowl pan juices. Sauté for a minute or so. Finally, stir in the herbs and serve.

SERVES 4

Serve with French Beans with Sesame Seeds *(see page 118)*

Chicken with apricots and potato straws

A traditional Parsi dish, this is always cooked at special occasions. The potato straws are a traditional Indian garnish. They don't act as an accompaniment – they aren't chips! – but instead add a wonderful crisp texture to the chicken. Serve with Saffron Rice for a fabulous meal for entertaining.

FOR THE CHICKEN

200g dried apricots
3 tomatoes, finely chopped
4 tbsp ghee or vegetable oil
2 x 2cm cinnamon sticks
2 onions, finely sliced
6 garlic cloves, crushed
5cm piece of root ginger, grated
600g boned chicken,
in 2cm cubes
juice of 1 lime or lemon
1 tbsp caster sugar
3 tbsp chopped coriander

FOR THE POTATO STRAWS

2 large potatoes, peeled and cut
into julienne
salt
¼ tsp turmeric
vegetable oil, to deep-fry
¼ tsp chilli powder
1 tsp finely chopped
coriander leaves

FOR THE MASALA

4–6 dried red chillies
1½ tsp cumin seeds
1 tbsp coriander seeds
5cm cinnamon stick, broken
into pieces
1 tsp green cardamom pods
6–8 cloves

Before you begin, soak the apricots in 250ml warm water for up to two hours. Remove half of them and blitz to a purée in a blender or food processor with 150ml of the soaking water. Reserve the remaining whole apricots and their soaking water. Set both aside.

Soak the potato julienne in water, with 2 tsp salt, for 15 minutes, to draw out the starch. Lightly salt the chopped tomatoes.

Now grind together all the ingredients for the masala in a coffee or spice grinder and set aside.

Heat the ghee or oil in a large, heavy-based pan until hot. Add the cinnamon sticks and allow to sizzle for a few seconds. Add the onions, garlic and ginger and cook until the onions turn golden brown. Now add the masala and sauté until the oil begins to separate from it. If the mixture begins to stick, add a dash of water and scrape the bottom of the pan. Continue to stir-fry for a couple of minutes, then add the tomatoes. Cook until the tomatoes have incorporated well, then add the chicken and the puréed apricots and sauté for another five minutes. Now add the whole apricots, with their soaking liquid. Bring to the boil, cover and simmer for about five minutes. Add the lime or lemon juice with the sugar, cover and continue to simmer for 10–15 minutes, until the chicken is tender. Stir in the coriander and adjust the seasoning.

Meanwhile, drain the potato julienne, spread out on a tea towel and pat dry. Mix with the turmeric. Heat the oil for deep-frying in a deep pan or wok until a potato straw sizzles as soon as it is added, then add the potato in batches. Fry until crisp and golden. Remove with a slotted spoon and drain on kitchen paper. Sprinkle with the chilli powder and fold in the chopped coriander.

Serve the chicken with the potato straws piled on top, or in a bowl alongside if you prefer.

SERVES 4

Serve with
Saffron Rice
(see page 134)

Stuffed quails with creamy sauce

Game was eaten a lot in Rajasthan, and this is a very rich, royal recipe. It is time-consuming, but it's worth the trouble for this opulent dish. All the prep can be done in advance, leaving you with just the job of roasting the birds on the day. If you want to impress guests at dinner and decide to glam up, this will definitely gild the game!

FOR THE STUFFING AND QUAILS

120g minced chicken breast
1 tbsp grated garlic and ginger
2 green chillies, finely chopped
1 tbsp raisins
1 tbsp chopped dried cherries
1 tbsp roasted cashew nuts
1 tbsp chopped pistachios
1 tbsp chopped coriander stalks
½ tsp ground cardamom
½ tsp ground cinnamon
1 star anise, finely ground
1¼ tsp garam masala
4 quail's eggs, cooked, shelled
4 boned quails (keep the bones)
4 tbsp melted butter
¼ tsp chilli powder

FOR THE SAUCE

4 tbsp vegetable oil
3–4 green cardamom pods
2 x 3cm cinnamon sticks
4 cloves and 1 tsp cumin seeds
2 bay leaves and 1 star anise
2 shallots, finely sliced
1 green chilli, finely chopped
½ tsp ground cinnamon
½ tsp ground cardamom
1–2 tbsp tomato purée
1 tbsp chopped coriander stalks
4–6 tbsp double cream
½ tsp garam masala

TO SERVE

4 tbsp vegetable oil or ghee
2 onions, finely sliced
2 tbsp chopped coriander

Put all the ingredients for the stuffing, down to and including the star anise, into a mixing bowl and add 1 tsp of the garam masala. Mix thoroughly and divide into four balls. Wrap the stuffing mixture around each quail's egg as if making Scotch eggs. Set aside.

Season the quails with salt and pepper and place a stuffing ball in the middle of the each. Wrap the legs over the filling, turn over, tuck everything in and shape it nice and tight. Cover and refrigerate for an hour or so to firm up.

In the meantime, make the sauce. Heat the oil in a pan over a medium-high heat and add all the whole spices. Once they begin to sizzle and splutter and their aroma is released, add the shallots and lightly sprinkle with salt. Sauté until they turn golden brown, then add the chilli. Stir-fry for a few seconds, then add the quail bones and ground spices and fry for a further two to three minutes. Now mix the tomato purée with 2 tbsp water and add it with the coriander stalks. Contine to stir-fry for a further minute, then add enough water to cover the bones. Bring to the boil, then reduce the heat and simmer until reduced by half. Strain the sauce through a sieve into a separate pan, then add the cream and garam masala and adjust the seasoning. Reheat gently to serve.

Preheat the oven to 200°C/400°F/gas mark 6 and return the birds to room temperature. Mix the melted butter with the chilli powder and ¼ tsp of the garam masala and use this to baste the quails. Roast for 30 minutes, or until cooked through. Baste the birds once more halfway through. Once the birds are cooked, rest for a few minutes.

In a separate frying pan, heat the oil or ghee to serve until hot and add the onions. Fry until golden brown, then drain on kitchen paper and sprinkle with some salt.

Spoon the sauce on to a deep platter and place the quails on top. Serve with the crispy fried onions and chopped coriander.

SERVES 4

Serve with
Jewelled Rice
(see page 135)

Duck breasts with orange, ginger and cinnamon

Duck with orange is a typical and deservedly classic French combination, but I have tinkered with the notion, mixing in ginger and cinnamon to create another of my beloved 'Frindian' dishes. The duck goes so perfectly with my celeriac gratin that it would be a tremendous shame not to make both. The sweetness of the celeriac and cinnamon flatter the sweet-sharpness of the duck and make it a perfect harmony of flavours. This would be a lovely alternative Christmas dish.

4 duck breasts, each 180–200g
2 tsp ground cinnamon
2 tsp ground allspice
½ tsp chilli flakes
salt
1 tbsp grated root ginger
finely grated zest of 1 orange, plus juice of 4, plus 4 more oranges cut into segments
4 tbsp maple syrup
1½ tbsp pomegranate molasses

Trim the silverskin from the duck breasts. Using a sharp knife, score the fat in a criss-cross pattern, taking care not to cut into the flesh.

Mix together the cinnamon, allspice, chilli flakes, salt, ginger and orange zest. Rub this mixture all over the duck breasts, massaging well. Put into a mixing bowl and cover with cling film. Allow to marinate for a few hours in the fridge.

Return the duck to room temperature while you preheat the oven to 200°C/400°F/gas mark 6.

Heat a wide, heavy-based ovenproof frying pan, or a cast-iron grill pan, over a low heat. Sprinkle some salt on the skin of the duck and place in the pan, skin side down. Cook until the fat has rendered and the skin is crisp. Spoon the excess fat from the pan, turn the breasts over and put into the oven. Roast for eight to 10 minutes, until the flesh is still pink in the middle. Allow to rest for three to five minutes.

Meanwhile, heat the orange juice, orange segments, maple syrup and pomegranate molasses with any juices that emerge from the duck. Reduce the liquid by half and adjust the seasoning. Thinly slice the duck breast on the diagonal and serve with the sauce.

SERVES 4

Serve with Celeriac Gratin with Cinnamon and Onion Confit *(see page 120)*

Stuffed haunch of venison

I am so delighted with this dish. It is truly festive and a great alternative to turkey at Christmas, with the usual trimmings (except bread sauce). A small slice of haunch goes a long way, as it is very rich. Do pay close attention to the cooking time and allow the meat to rest; there's nothing worse than overcooked venison, which is like tough old boots. No doubt yours will melt like velvet!

FOR THE SPICE MIX

1 tsp whole pink peppercorns
1 tsp juniper berries
3 star anise
12–15 green cardamom pods
1 tsp allspice berries
1 cinnamon stick, broken up
salt

FOR THE VENISON

1 haunch of venison, boned, weighing 1.45kg, well trimmed, removing fat and sinews
300ml orange juice

FOR THE STUFFING

2 tbsp vegetable oil, plus more to sear the meat
1 large onion, finely chopped
4 garlic cloves, crushed
1 green chilli, finely chopped
80g dried cherries
60g dried cranberries
60g raisins
50 dried apricots, finely chopped
50g walnuts, finely chopped
3 tbsp chopped flat leaf parsley leaves
2 tbsp chopped coriander leaves

FOR THE GRAVY

420ml chicken or game stock, made with pink peppercorns, juniper and cinnamon, if you like
100ml port
1 tbsp redcurrant jelly

Coarsely grind all the spices for the spice mix in a coffee grinder or mortar and pestle. Rub the spice mix and some salt all over the haunch, massage well and set aside. Heat the oil for the stuffing over a medium heat and add the onion. Sauté until it begins to caramelise, then add the garlic and chilli. Stir for a minute or so, then add the fruits and walnuts and stir for a few seconds, until the mixture glistens and the berries plump up. Remove from the heat, stir in the herbs and adjust the seasoning. Allow to cool.

Spread the haunch flat on a board, flesh side up, and pack the cool filling where the bone would have been, making an even layer. Roll the meat around the stuffing. Tie the joint at 2.5cm intervals with kitchen string as neatly as possible. Place on a roasting tin, then pour over the orange juice. Refrigerate for at least 24 hours, turning at regular intervals. Remove the haunch from the fridge around one hour before cooking to bring to room temperature. Preheat the oven to 180°C/350°F/gas mark 4.

Remove the venison from its marinade and lightly pat dry. Using tongs, sear the meat in 1–2 tbsp of oil on all sides, browning well, on a griddle or frying pan. Return to the roasting tin with the marinade and place in the oven. Roast for 12 minutes per 500g for medium-rare (just pink in the middle), or 10 minutes per 500g for rarer. Remove from the oven, cover with foil and rest in a warm place for 20 minutes, to allow the juices to settle back into the meat.

Meanwhile, make the gravy. Remove any excess fat from the juices in the roasting tin, add the stock and deglaze, scraping off the caramelised bits from the bottom of the tin. Pour in the port and reduce until you have one-third of the amount of liquid you started with, or until you reach the desired intensity. Strain into a clean pan, then stir in the redcurrant jelly. Cut the strings from the meat and carve into thick slices. Any juices can be poured back into the gravy.

SERVES 6

Serve with **Roast Potatoes** *or* **Parsnips with Chilli and Chaat Masala** *(see page 115)*

Indian high tea

A beautiful spread for a celebration. Indians love grazing, they love tea and they love really sweet things. I have cut back the sugar here as I don't share that passion. Leave it out of the tea if you want, too, it will still be delicious. The halva is a super-quick cake; very handy to have in your repertoire when you need a pud but have run out of time.

Crab samosas

1 tbsp vegetable oil
1½ tsp black mustard seeds
6–8 curry leaves, shredded
½ onion, finely chopped
1 tsp turmeric
2cm piece of root ginger, grated
250g crab meat
2 tbsp grated fresh coconut
2 tsp finely chopped green or red chillies
2 tbsp finely chopped coriander leaves
squeeze of lemon or lime juice
salt
125g unsalted butter
270g filo pastry
rock salt and cumin seeds, to sprinkle

Heat the oil in a wide frying pan until hot, then add the mustard seeds. Once they begin to pop, add the curry leaves, onion and turmeric and sauté until the onion becomes soft and translucent. Add the ginger and stir-fry for a minute or so. Now add the crab, coconut and chillies. Cook until all the moisture has gone, then add the coriander and lemon juice. Cook for a further minute, then remove from the heat and allow to cool, seasoning to taste with salt.

Preheat the oven to 200°C/400°F/gas mark 6. Melt the butter. Lay a sheet of filo on a work surface and brush with butter. Place a second sheet on top to fit exactly over the first. Now cut the filo into strips about 5cm wide. Spoon about 1 heaped tsp of filling into one corner of the strip. Fold the right corner of the strip over to the left side, to create a triangle. Continue to fold the triangle along the strip until you reach the end, cutting off any surplus pastry. Repeat until you have used up all the pastry and filling. Brush the samosas liberally with butter and sprinkle with rock salt and cumin seeds. Bake in the oven for 10–12 minutes, until golden.

MAKES ABOUT 24

Masala tea

2 bay leaves
1 cinnamon stick
5 cardamom pods
5 cloves
4 black peppercorns
1 slice of root ginger
3 heaped tbsp Ceylon tea leaves
75ml evaporated milk
caster sugar, to taste

Pour 1 litre of cold water into a saucepan and add the bay, cinnamon, cardamom, cloves and peppercorns. Bring to a boil over a high heat. Add the ginger and cook for another two minutes, then add the tea leaves. Return to the boil and cook for one minute, then reduce the heat to a minimum and allow to steep for around two minutes. If you like strong tea, leave it for a further five minutes. Add the evaporated milk and sugar to taste and strain into a cup or teapot ready to serve.

SERVES 4

Sweet potato cakes

2 tbsp vegetable oil, plus more
to shallow-fry
1 tsp cumin seeds
1 tsp fennel seeds
½ tsp chilli powder
1 tsp garam masala
1 tsp crushed garlic
1 tsp grated root ginger
1 long red chilli, finely chopped
100g shredded spinach
400g cooked floury potatoes,
roughly mashed
200g cooked sweet potatoes,
roughly mashed
salt
freshly ground black pepper
150g paneer, crumbled
1 tbsp chopped coriander leaves
plain flour, to dust

Heat the 2 tbsp of oil in a frying pan until smoking, then add the cumin and fennel seeds. When they begin to crackle, add the chilli powder, garam masala, garlic, ginger and red chilli. Stir for one to two minutes.

Now add the spinach and stir until completely coated in the spice mixture. Remove from the heat when the spinach begins to wilt; it will continue to cook in the heat of the pan.

Place the two types of potato into a large mixing bowl and add the spiced spinach mixture. Mix well, season generously, then add the paneer and coriander. Mould into small cakes and dust with flour.

Place the cakes in the fridge to firm up for about an hour, then shallow-fry in hot oil for two to three minutes on each side, or until piping hot all the way through. Drain well on kitchen paper and serve.

MAKES 10–12

Saffron halva with pistachio

½ tsp saffron threads
450ml whole milk
30g raisins
90g unsalted butter, plus more
for the tin
150g caster sugar
150g semolina
80g shelled, unsalted
pistachios, slivered

Put the saffron in a cup. Heat 2 tbsp of the milk, add to the saffron and soak for 15–20 minutes. Put the raisins in a bowl and cover with warm water. Lightly butter a 20cm cake tin. Heat the remaining milk with the sugar until it dissolves and pour in the saffron milk.

In a separate pan, melt the butter and cook for a few minutes, then add the semolina. Stir over a low heat until the semolina turns golden brown. Now pour in the warm milk and stir vigorously until it comes away from the sides of the pan. It should be smooth; if it's at all gritty, add more milk and cook for a bit longer.

Add the pistachios and drained raisins, then pour into the tin. Pack down, cover and leave in a warm place for 10–15 minutes. Serve with clotted cream, yogurt, or simply on its own!

SERVES 4–6

Classic
CURRIES

Spinach koftas in tomato sauce

Deep-frying is simply to create a crust. This dish won't be oily, but light and bursting with flavour. The sauce can be made well in advance. And the answer to the long ingredients list? Like any good Girl Guide: be prepared. You can serve these with the sauce on the side as a dip, as in the photo, or drop the koftas into the sauce and serve immediately as a lovely veggie main.

FOR THE SAUCE

1kg tomatoes, quartered
2 garlic cloves, chopped
2.5cm piece of root ginger, grated
3 green cardamom pods
5 cloves
1 bay leaf
2 tsp chilli powder
1 tsp ground cinnamon
75g unsalted butter, chilled and diced
100ml single cream
salt
1 tsp dried fenugreek leaves, crushed
½ tsp garam masala
1–2 tsp caster sugar, to taste

FOR THE KOFTAS

250g paneer, grated
1 large potato, cooked and grated (250g prepared weight)
200g spinach leaves, shredded
2.5cm piece of root ginger, finely chopped
2 green chillies, deseeded if you like, finely chopped
½ tsp ajowain (carom) seeds
vegetable oil, to deep-fry

FOR THE BATTER

100g gram flour
½ tsp ajwain (carom) seeds
1–2 tsp amchur (mango powder)
½ tsp salt

To make the sauce, put the tomatoes into a large saucepan. Cover and cook over a medium heat until they begin to soften. Add 125ml of water, the garlic, ginger, cardamom, cloves and bay leaf. Bring to the boil, reduce the heat and simmer until the tomatoes disintegrate.

Remove and liquidise in a blender. Strain if necessary, then pour into a clean saucepan, add the chilli powder and cinnamon and simmer for 10 minutes, until slightly thickened. Add the butter a little at a time, stirring constantly. When the sauce turns glossy, add the cream and simmer for a couple of minutes. Season with salt, stir in the fenugreek and garam masala and add sugar to bring out the flavours. Set aside.

To make the koftas, put all the ingredients except the oil into a bowl and mix well. Shape into balls, each the size of golf balls.

To make the batter, put the gram flour, spices and salt into another bowl and make a well in the centre. Gradually stir in 70ml iced water to achieve a smooth batter with the consistency of single cream.

Heat the oil either in a deep-fat fryer or a deep saucepan until hot. Dip the koftas into the batter, then check whether the oil is hot by sprinkling a tiny bit of the batter into the oil. If it sizzles immediately, the oil is ready. Add the koftas and fry for 1½ minutes, turning once, until crisp and golden. Drain on kitchen paper. Serve with the warm tomato sauce.

SERVES 6

Serve with **Perfect Rice** *(see page 132), and* **Gingered Carrots with Maple Syrup** *(see page 125)*

Buttermilk sweet potato and beans

This dish is absolutely sublime, with its south Indian flavours of mustard seeds and curry leaves. It is incredibly vibrant, with its beautiful orange and bright green tones. It really comes together when you add the cashew nuts. Best of all, this is a truly simple dish and doesn't take long to make at all.

30g broken cashew nuts
30g melon seeds
550g sweet potatoes, peeled and cut into 1.5cm cubes
200g French beans, de-stringed and cut into 2.5cm lengths
salt
30g freshly grated coconut, or 15g desiccated coconut, soaked in warm water and squeezed dry
½ tsp turmeric
1 tbsp grated root ginger
2 green chillies, deseeded if you like
450ml buttermilk
2 tbsp vegetable oil
2 tbsp light sesame oil
1 tsp black mustard seeds
1 tsp cumin seeds
3–4 dried red chillies
10–12 curry leaves
generous handful of spinach, shredded
2–3 tbsp chopped coriander leaves

Put the cashew nuts and melon seeds into a bowl and pour over hot water from the kettle. Leave to soak for 15 minutes, then drain.

Separately blanch both the sweet potatoes and the French beans in boiling salted water. The sweet potatoes will need five minutes, and the beans just two to three minutes. Drain and refresh in cold water. Set aside.

In a jug blender, grind together the nuts, melon seeds, coconut, turmeric, ginger, chillies, salt to taste and enough of the buttermilk to make a very smooth paste.

In a separate pan, heat both the oils over a medium heat until hot. Add the mustard and cumin seeds and the dried chillies. Once they crackle and pop and the chillies have turned a shade darker, add the curry leaves and the nut mixture and stir-fry for a minute or so.

Reduce the heat and pour in the remainder of the buttermilk, the sweet potatoes, green beans and spinach. Simmer for a few minutes, until the spinach wilts, then adjust the seasoning. Sprinkle over the chopped coriander and serve.

SERVES 4

Serve with
Coconut Rice
(see page 132)

Broad beans with yogurt, garlic and dill

This is a very creamy dish and handy to have in your repertoire, as broad beans are available throughout the year, either fresh or frozen. You can add some baby spinach leaves at the end to give some contrast, if you prefer. Because it is coated in a yogurty sauce, it is great with grilled meats, especially lamb chops.

1 head of garlic
3 tbsp rapeseed or vegetable oil, plus more for the garlic
1.2kg fresh or frozen broad beans
½ tsp asafoetida
2 tsp salt
1 tsp ground cumin
1 tsp ground black pepper
1 tsp caster sugar
½ tsp turmeric
2 tbsp lime juice
30g dill, chopped
2 green chillies, finely chopped
200g Greek yogurt
2–3 tbsp chopped coriander leaves

Preheat the oven to 180°C/350°F/gas mark 4. Slice the stalk end from the head of garlic and place on to a square of foil large enough to wrap around the bulb. Drizzle with oil and cook in the hot oven for 45 minutes, or until the bulb is tender when squeezed. Squeeze from the base over a small bowl, pushing out all the sweet, melting garlic flesh. Set aside.

If you are using fresh broad beans, first pod them and then skin the beans. For frozen beans, soak in warm water for about five minutes before skinning the beans.

Heat the 3 tbsp of oil in a wok or deep frying pan over a medium heat until very hot, and add the asafoetida. Stir-fry for a minute, then add the beans, salt, cumin, pepper, sugar, turmeric and lime juice. Stir-fry for about five minutes.

Add 150ml of water and bring to the boil. Reduce the heat, cover and simmer over a medium-low heat for 15–20 minutes, or until the beans are tender, adding a dash more water if needed. Add the dill, green chillies, roast garlic pulp and yogurt and simmer for a further eight to 10 minutes. Adjust the seasoning and finish off with the chopped coriander.

SERVES 4 AS A SIDE DISH

Serve with
Tandoori Lamb
Racks *(see page 104)*

Prawns in tomato and coconut milk

This is a very south Indian dish, with its use of coconut and tomatoes, and actually very simple to make. If you only have cooked prawns, add them right at the end of cooking, just to heat through. Try to get raw prawns though, as the flavour will be exquisite. Once the sauce has been passed through the sieve and returned to the pan, make sure it is only cooked over a gentle heat, so the coconut milk doesn't split.

500g raw prawns, peeled and
deveined, retaining the
tail shells
salt
¾ tsp turmeric
juice of 1 lime or lemon
2 tbsp vegetable oil
1 tsp black mustard seeds
1 tsp cumin seeds
a few curry leaves
1 tsp crushed garlic
1 tsp finely chopped root ginger
1 green chilli, finely chopped
4 kaffir lime leaves, shredded
1 shallot, thinly sliced
200ml fish stock
100ml tomato passata
½ tsp chilli powder
pinch of caster sugar
400ml coconut milk
1 tbsp chopped coriander
leaves, plus more to serve

Peel, devein and rinse the prawns. Mix them with salt to taste, ¼ tsp of the turmeric and half the lime or lemon juice, and leave to marinate for 10–15 minutes.

Meanwhile, heat the oil in a pan until hot and add the mustard and cumin seeds. Once they begin to pop and splutter, add the curry leaves, garlic, ginger, chilli, lime leaves and shallot. Reduce the heat slightly and cook until the shallot becomes translucent. Now add the remaining turmeric and stir-fry for a few seconds, then add the stock, bring to the boil and cook for three to four minutes, until it has reduced. Now add the passata, chilli powder and sugar. Reduce further until it has a consistency you like, then add the coconut milk and coriander, taste, adjust the seasoning and simmer for five minutes or so.

Remove the sauce from the heat and pass through a fine sieve, then return it to the pan. Bring to a simmer over a gentle heat, then add the prawns. Cook on a low heat for five to seven minutes, until the prawns turn pink and are just cooked. Finish off with the remaining lemon or lime juice and sprinkle with coriander to serve.

SERVES 4

Serve with
Coconut Rice
(see page 132)

Tandoori king prawns

These are a perennial favourite. The flavour of the mustard oil and ajwain (carom) seeds is wonderfully intense. The secret of tandoori dishes lies mostly in the marinade, which does everything for you. There's not much for the cook to do... you could always have a cup of tea and tackle a spot of ironing while the prawns are marinating, I suppose.

FOR THE FIRST MARINADE
½ heaped tbsp grated garlic
½ heaped tbsp grated root ginger
1 tsp turmeric
1½ tsp chilli powder
juice of 1 lemon
1 tbsp mustard oil mixed with
1 tbsp rapeseed or vegetable oil
salt

FOR THE PRAWNS
800g raw king prawns, peeled and deveined, retaining the tail shells

FOR THE SECOND MARINADE
2–3 tbsp thick yogurt
1 tbsp mustard oil mixed with
1 tbsp rapeseed or vegetable oil
1 tsp ajwain (carom) seeds or 1 tsp ground black mustard seeds
½ tsp garam masala

In a large mixing bowl, combine all the ingredients for the first marinade with the prawns and leave to marinate for 30 minutes in the fridge.

Mix all the ingredients for the second marinade and add to the prawns. Leave in the fridge for a further hour.

Thread the prawns on to skewers, if you like, and place under a hot grill, or on a barbecue, or in a hot griddle pan. Cook on both sides just until the prawns turn pink and are cooked through.

SERVES 4–6

Photo shows Tandoori King Prawns *(left) and* Beef Tikkas *(right, see page 100)*

Serve with Beansprout Salad with Chargrilled sparagus and Coconut *(see page 116)*

Prawns in chilli sauce

This recipe is a classic Goan dish, combining that state's essential use of vinegar with a spectrum of spices. You probably already have these spices in your cupboards... go and have a look now, I'm sure they'll be there! If you prefer not to use vinegar, you can substitute a little more lemon or lime juice as a souring agent.

FOR THE PRAWNS
juice of ½ lemon or lime
salt
1 tsp chilli powder
1 tsp turmeric
1kg medium raw prawns, peeled and deveined
3 tbsp vegetable oil
6 garlic cloves, crushed or grated
2 onions, finely chopped
6–8 tomatoes, finely chopped
1 tbsp tomato purée
1 tbsp chopped coriander leaves

FOR THE SPICE PASTE
1 tsp cumin seeds
1 tbsp coriander seeds
½ tsp black peppercorns
4 cloves
1 x 2.5cm cinnamon stick
seeds from 4 green cardamom pods
1 bay leaf
6 whole dried chillies
2.5cm piece of root ginger, grated
6 garlic cloves, roughly chopped
1–2 tsp caster sugar
1 tsp turmeric
2 tbsp cider vinegar, plus more if needed

Rub the lemon juice, salt, chilli powder and turmeric into the prawns and leave for a few minutes to marinate.

Blend all the ingredients for the spice paste in a blender or liquidiser until very smooth. (Add a little more vinegar if necessary, instead of water, to give a smooth consistency.) Remove and set aside.

Heat the oil in a wide pan, add the garlic and onions and cook until the onions begin to change colour. Add the spice paste and stir-fry for a few minutes until the paste has mellowed out. Now add the tomatoes and tomato purée and cook for a further four or five minutes, until they have thoroughly incorporated into the sauce. It should be a thick coating consistency, but thin it out with water if it's too thick for you.

Finally add the prawns and cook until just pink and cooked through. Adjust the seasoning, sprinkle with the chopped coriander and serve.

SERVES 4

Serve with
Coconut Rice
(see page 132)

Red fish curry

This has a complex taste, both piquant and aromatic. It is on the spicy side, but the coconut milk helps to tame the heat. If you are going to be using a lot of grated garlic or root ginger, it's a good idea to make a big batch in advance and freeze it in freezer bags. Simply grate a large amount of garlic or ginger – or, even quicker, blitz it in a food processor with a little vegetable oil and water to help form a smooth paste – then freeze. Bash a bit off with a rolling pin and defrost to use as needed.

10 Kashmiri dried chillies, 5 deseeded and 5 left whole
1 tsp cumin seeds
1 tsp sesame seeds
1 tsp coriander seeds
3 cloves
6–8 peppercorns
2.5cm cinnamon stick or cassia bark
3 green cardamom pods
1 tbsp grated root ginger
4 garlic cloves, grated
2 onions, finely chopped
100ml fish stock, plus more for the paste (optional)
4 tbsp vegetable oil
2 tomatoes, finely chopped
1 tbsp tomato purée, diluted in a small amount of water
400ml can coconut milk
4 x sea bass fillets, each 160–180g
juice of ½ lime
salt
1 tbsp finely chopped coriander leaves

Soak the Kashmiri chillies in a small amount of warm water for at least 20 minutes, to soften.

In a small dry frying pan, lightly roast the cumin, sesame and coriander seeds, the cloves, peppercorns, cinnamon or cassia and cardamom over a medium-low heat, until the spices release their aromas. Put into a coffee or spice grinder and blend to a fine powder.

Put the ginger, garlic, onions and drained chillies into a jug blender and blend to a smooth paste, adding about 100ml of water or fish stock to achieve a smooth paste. Add the roasted, ground spice mixture and mix thoroughly.

Heat the oil in a wide, heavy-based pan over a medium-high heat. Add the onion paste and the 100ml of stock and stir-fry for eight to 10 minutes, until the mixture mellows out and the moisture has evaporated to leave a thick paste. Add the tomatoes and tomato purée and continue to cook until all the tomatoes have disintegrated into the sauce.

Add the coconut milk, bring to the boil, reduce the heat and simmer. Add the fish fillets and cook for five to eight minutes, until the fish begins to flake. Squeeze in the lime juice, adjust the seasoning, and sprinkle with the chopped coriander.

SERVES 4

Serve with
Perfect Rice
(see page 132)

Fish koftas

The flavours here are intense yet delicate and the sauce a beautiful orange colour from the saffron. The sauce can be served separately, as a dip, or the koftas can be mixed into the sauce and served with Saffron Rice.

FOR THE SAUCE

3 tbsp ghee
1 black cardamom pod, crushed
1 large onion, finely sliced
1 tbsp grated root ginger
½ tsp turmeric
2 tsp ground cumin
½ tsp chilli powder
1 tsp garam masala
6 tomatoes, liquidised
pinch of saffron threads steeped in 1 tbsp hot milk
salt
8 tbsp yogurt whisked with 2 tbsp water

FOR THE FISH

240ml whole milk
4–6 green cardamom pods, lightly crushed
1 black cardamom pod
¼ tsp turmeric
¼ tsp ground cumin
500g white fish fillets, rinsed and patted dry
1 large potato, cooked and diced
1 onion, roughly chopped
1 tsp roughly chopped root ginger
1 large green chilli
2–3 tbsp chopped coriander leaves, plus more to serve
1 tsp roasted cumin seeds, coarsely crushed
2 tbsp flaked almonds, toasted, plus more to serve
1 tbsp gram flour
freshly ground black pepper
1 egg, beaten
vegetable oil, to deep-fry

For the sauce, heat the ghee in a heavy-based saucepan over a medium heat. Add the cardamom and onion and cook until the onion turns a pale gold. Now add the ginger and stir-fry for a few seconds, then add the turmeric, cumin, chilli powder and garam masala and continue to stir-fry for a few minutes, allowing the ghee to separate. If the mixture starts to stick to the pan, add a dash of water and continue to stir-fry for a few more seconds. Add the tomatoes, the saffron and its milk and salt to taste, then stir and simmer for a couple more minutes. Gradually add the yogurt and simmer for a further three to four minutes. Squeeze out the seeds from the cardamom pod and discard the husk. Pour the sauce into a blender and liquidise until smooth.

Now, for the fish, bring the milk, cardamom pods, turmeric and ground cumin to the boil in a heavy-based pan. Poach the fish fillets in this for three minutes on either side, drain, discarding the milk, and transfer to a mixing bowl. Leave to cool. Now remove the cardamom pods and add the potato.

Blend the onion, ginger and green chilli with 1 tbsp of water to a smooth paste in a liquidiser. Add this to the fish mixture along with all the other ingredients except the oil. Knead well together and form into balls, each the size of a ping-pong ball. (If the mixture is sticky, moisten your hands with water before forming the koftas.)

Heat the oil for deep-frying in a deep, heavy-based pan or wok until it begins to sizzle. Reduce the heat and drop the fish balls into the oil a few at a time, turning them frequently and frying to an even golden brown. Drain on kitchen paper.

Put the koftas into a dish and pour the reheated sauce over. Sprinkle with coriander and almonds and serve.

SERVES 4

Serve with **Saffron Rice** *(see page 134)*

Chicken in a cashew nut sauce

If you want prosperity on a plate, do as the Moghuls did and cook with cashew nuts, as they were a very expensive ingredient designed to impress. This has a nice medium heat to it and the richness of the sauce is a complete delight; one for the chilli weaklings! When you are grinding the spice and cashew mixture, make sure the paste is very smooth, as the sauce may look curdled if it's not finely ground. Serve it with colourful vegetables to add a few more tones and textures.

250g cashew nuts
100g vegetable oil
2 onions, chopped, plus
½ onion, finely sliced
12 garlic cloves
2.5cm piece of root ginger, chopped
2½ tbsp coriander seeds
1½ tsp cumin seeds
4 dried red chillies
6 cloves
8cm cinnamon stick
100g freshly grated coconut
salt
2 green chillies, finely chopped
1kg boneless chicken thighs and legs, cut into 5cm pieces
3 tbsp yogurt

Before you start, put 100g of the cashew nuts into a bowl and add just enough warm water to soak them. Leave for two hours. Drain and place them in a blender or food processor, adding a little warm water. Blitz to a thick, smooth paste. Set aside.

Place 25g more of the cashew nuts in a small frying pan and stir over a medium heat until toasted. Set aside.

Heat a small amount of the oil in the same pan and cook the sliced onion until crisp. Drain on kitchen paper and set aside.

In a large frying pan, dry-roast the garlic, ginger, coriander seeds, cumin seeds, dried chillies, cloves and cinnamon over a low heat for five minutes, stirring. Add the coconut, 75g more of the cashew nuts and the chopped onions and roast for 10 minutes more, stirring all the time. Remove from the heat and leave to cool. Grind the mixture either in a blender or food processor, adding 150–250ml water, to a very smooth consistency.

Heat the remaining oil in a wide cooking pot, add the blended spice mixture and fry for 10 minutes over a low heat. Add the ground cashew paste with some salt and fry for two minutes, adding the green chillies.

Increase the heat to medium-high, and add the chicken pieces. Fry for five minutes, then add the remaining untoasted cashews. Stir-fry for a minute or so, then add 600ml of water. Bring to the boil, reduce the heat and simmer for 10–15 minutes, until the chicken is tender and cooked through.

Serve with a dollop of yogurt, the reserved toasted cashew nuts and the crispy fried onions.

SERVES 4–6

Serve with **Spinach with Radish Greens** *(see page 129)*

Chicken in a coriander and coconut sauce

This is such a lovely recipe. It comes from the Nilgiri hills in the westernmost point of Tamil Nadu. Due to the wonderful flora of the hills, the dish is verdant, with a delightful herb sauce that is an intense, vibrant green. We have served this recipe at the Star for some time and it remains a very popular choice.

2 tbsp cashew nuts
400g chopped coriander leaves and stalks
6 green chillies
250ml coconut milk
3–4 tbsp ghee or vegetable oil
2 onions, finely chopped
salt
¼ tsp turmeric
4 garlic cloves, crushed
4cm piece of root ginger, grated
½ tsp ground cumin
½ tsp ground coriander
½ tsp chilli powder
1kg boneless chicken breasts or thighs, or a combination of both
½ tsp garam masala
juice of ½ lemon or lime

Soak the cashew nuts in 100ml hot water for 15 minutes, then drain.

Blend together the chopped coriander, chillies, cashew nuts and coconut milk in a food processor or blender until it becomes a smooth paste. Decant into a bowl and set aside.

Heat the ghee or oil over a medium heat in a wide, heavy-based saucepan until hot. Add the onions with a pinch of salt and the turmeric. Cook until they become soft and not browned. (It will affect the colour of the dish if the onions are browned.)

Add the garlic and ginger and cook for a minute to allow them to mellow out. Now add the ground cumin, coriander and chilli powder. Stir-fry for up to three minutes, then add the coriander paste.

Cook for a few minutes, then add the chicken. Bring to the boil, reduce the heat and simmer for 12–15 minutes, until the chicken is tender and cooked through. Sprinkle with the garam masala, add the lemon or lime juice, adjust the seasoning and serve.

SERVES 4–6

Serve with
Coconut Rice
(see page 132)

Spinach and apricot stuffed chicken with yogurt sauce

Here's a chance to practise the art of transformation, creating eye-catching, dramatic medallions from the humble chicken breast. The stuffing bursts with colour and complex flavour, framed by succulent meat and a delicate, creamy sauce. The sauce and stuffing can be made in advance, then it's just an assembly job on the day. As the sauce is quite rich, you don't need much with it, perhaps just the light Colourful Spiced Cabbage.

FOR THE STUFFING

2 tbsp ghee or rapeseed oil
1 tsp cumin seeds
4 garlic cloves, grated
1 large red onion, finely chopped
1 tbsp grated root ginger
2 green chillies, finely chopped
300g spinach, shredded
1 tsp ground cinnamon
½ tsp ground nutmeg
75g dried apricots, chopped
75g grated paneer or ricotta
50g pine nuts, toasted

FOR THE CHICKEN

4 skinless chicken breasts
1 tsp crushed garlic
1 tsp grated root ginger
½ tsp ground cinnamon
½ tsp ground cardamom
1 tsp chilli powder or flakes
2–3 tbsp ghee or rapeseed oil

FOR THE SAUCE

4 tbsp ghee or rapeseed oil
2 onions, finely sliced
1 tbsp grated root ginger
3 tomatoes, deseeded and diced
1 tsp chilli powder
1 tsp ground cinnamon
150g yogurt
1 tsp garam masala
1–2 tbsp single cream
½ tsp caster sugar, or to taste

Prepare the stuffing. Heat a heavy-based pan and add the oil. When hot, add the cumin seeds and allow to crackle. Add the garlic and onion and sauté until very soft and starting to change colour. Add the ginger, chillies and spinach. Cook on a high heat until the liquid has evaporated. Add the cinnamon and nutmeg and stir in the apricots. Allow to cool, then stir in the cheese, pine nuts and salt to taste.

Slice each breast in half horizontally with a sharp knife, keeping one side joined, then open it out like a book. Flatten evenly with a rolling pin. Place each on a piece of cling film large enough to wrap around the breasts. Smear on both sides with garlic and ginger and sprinkle with salt, cinnamon, cardamom and chilli powder. Divide the stuffing into four portions and put one on each breast. Fold the chicken in from both sides, then roll up like a sausage. Wrap the cling film round tightly. Poach in simmering water for five to seven minutes, then drain.

For the sauce, heat the ghee or oil in a pan over a medium-high heat until hot and add the onions. Fry with a pinch of salt until they turn pale gold. Add the ginger and cook for a couple of minutes, then add the tomatoes, chilli powder and cinnamon. Continue to cook for a few minutes until the tomatoes have softened. Whisk in the yogurt with the garam masala and continue to cook on a low heat for two to three minutes, until the oil starts to separate out on top. Add the cream and adjust the seasoning with salt and sugar to taste.

Heat the ghee or oil for the chicken in a frying pan until hot, remove the chicken from the cling film and add to the pan. Sear on all sides, turning, to create an even golden colour. Rest for five minutes, then cut into slices and serve with the warm sauce.

SERVES 4

Serve with Colourful Spiced Cabbage *(see page 128)*

Black pepper chicken

In medieval Europe, black pepper was kept under lock and key, because of its high scarcity value. Now we can afford to liberate the peppercorns! Cooking with Indian spices is like alchemy: the other spices here make the black pepper in the recipe come alive, bringing a mouthwatering magic.

FOR THE PEPPER MASALA
1 tbsp black peppercorns
¼ tsp cardamom seeds
¼ tsp whole cloves
¼ tsp ground cinnamon

FOR THE CHICKEN
2 tsp grated root ginger
3 garlic cloves, crushed
¼ tsp turmeric
2 tbsp cider vinegar
salt
800g skinless and boneless chicken thighs, in 3cm cubes
4 tbsp vegetable oil
1 tsp cumin seeds
2 bay leaves
2.5cm cinnamon stick
4 cloves
4 green cardamom pods
1 tsp black peppercorns
3 onions, finely sliced
1 tomato, finely chopped
2 tbsp chopped coriander leaves
2 green chillies, slit

Grind all the ingredients for the pepper masala in a coffee or spice grinder to form a fine powder.

Mix the pepper masala with the ginger, garlic, turmeric, vinegar and salt to taste in a bowl and add the chicken. Cover and leave to marinate in the fridge for two hours.

Heat the oil in a deep pan over a medium heat. Add the cumin seeds and, as soon as they crackle, add the bay leaves, cinnamon, cloves, cardamom pods and peppercorns. Add the onions and fry until golden brown. Now add the tomato and continue to cook until thoroughly incorporated into the onion mixture.

Add the marinated chicken and sauté for a few minutes to allow the natural juices of the chicken to evaporate. Add just enough water – about 150ml – to cook the chicken. Bring to the boil, reduce the heat and braise for about 15 minutes, uncovered. When almost cooked, adjust the seasoning with salt and add the coriander. Finally, add the slit green chillies and serve.

SERVES 4

Serve with **Perfect Rice** *(see page 132), and* **Buttermilk, Sweet Potato and Beans** *(see page 82)*

Spicy chicken masala

Yes I know, I have given you a lengthy list of ingredients yet again! But these are mostly spices and all must-haves for the kitchen pantry. This is a spicy, piquant and tasty dish. For the chilli weaklings, deseed the chillies, to reduce the heat. Otherwise, have courage and enjoy this flavoursome recipe. The chicken does give a fiery kick, but the subtlety of all the spices still filter through.

1 tsp fennel seeds
1 tsp coriander seeds
½ tsp black peppercorns
1½ tsp cumin seeds
1½ tbsp grated root ginger
6–8 garlic cloves, crushed or grated
2–3 green chillies, roughly chopped, plus 4 green chillies, slit lengthways
1 tsp chilli powder
3 tbsp yogurt
salt
850g chicken thighs (about 8 thighs)
6 tbsp ghee or vegetable oil, plus more if needed
2 onions, thinly sliced
½ tsp turmeric
6 cardamom pods
3 cloves
1 cinnamon stick or cassia bark
300g ripe tomatoes, quartered
juice of ½ lemon
2 tbsp roughly chopped coriander leaves

Lightly toast the fennel and coriander seeds, the peppercorns and ½ tsp of the cumin seeds in a small frying pan until they release their aroma and turn a shade darker. Place in a coffee or spice grinder and grind to a fine powder. Transfer to a mini blender. Add the ginger, garlic, roughly chopped chillies, chilli powder, yogurt and salt to taste. Blend to a paste.

Place the chicken in a mixing bowl and rub the mixture thoroughly over the meat. Cover with cling film and put in the fridge for up to two hours.

In a wide pan, large enough to accommodate all the thighs in a single layer, heat the ghee or oil over a medium-high heat until hot. Add the onions and tumeric and fry until the onions turn golden brown, then remove the onions with a slotted spoon and drain on kitchen paper. Once cooled, blend the onions, either in a blender or food processor, to a coarse, paste-like consistency. Set aside.

Reheat the ghee or oil in which the onions have been fried over a medium-high heat until hot. It is likely this will be sufficient for the next stage of cooking, but add a little more oil if required. Add the cardamom, cloves, cinnamon or cassia and remaining cumin seeds. Fry for a few seconds until they begin to sizzle. Add the chicken thighs in a single layer and lightly brown the meat on both sides. Add 250ml of water, bring to the boil then reduce the heat to low. Add the slit chillies and two-thirds of the tomatoes. Cover and cook at a simmer for 20–25 minutes, until tender and cooked through.

Squeeze over the lemon juice. Add the remaining tomatoes and the chopped coriander. Heat through so that the tomatoes just soften, but retain their shape. Serve with a dollop of yogurt.

SERVES 4

Serve with **Saffron Rice** *(see page 134)*

Beef tikkas

The term tikka simply means boneless pieces of meat, traditionally cooked in a tandoor oven. Tandoori dishes are marinated for several hours, so the flavours penetrate the meat and break down the fibres, meaning it doesn't take long to cook. You still get an amazing richness of flavour even from a brief cooking time. This is great cooked on a barbecue as well. Mustard oil has a very intense flavour, but just leave it out if you can't find it. I like to mix mustard oil with vegetable oil, in a ratio of 2:1, to round out the taste. For a photo, see page 86.

FOR THE BEEF
900g rump steak, cut into 3cm cubes

FOR THE FIRST MARINADE
1 tbsp grated root ginger
1 tbsp grated garlic
1–2 tsp freshly ground black pepper
juice of 1 lemon
1 tsp salt

FOR THE SECOND MARINADE
1 tsp cumin seeds
1 tsp fennel seeds
120ml vegetable oil, plus 1 tbsp
1 large onion, thinly sliced, plus 1 medium onion, chopped
4–6 tbsp yogurt
3 tbsp mustard oil
1 tbsp ground almonds
2–3 green chillies, deseeded if you like, roughly chopped
1 tsp ground coriander
½ tsp garam masala
salt

Put the beef in a mixing bowl and add all the ingredients for the first marinade. Mix, cover and refrigerate for two hours.

Meanwhile, put the cumin and fennel seeds in a small frying pan, place over a medium heat and stir until they smell aromatic. Pour into a mortar and grind to a powder with the pestle.

Pour the 120ml of vegetable oil into a pan and set over a medium-high heat. Once the oil is hot, add the sliced onion and fry until golden brown. Remove with a slotted spoon and drain on kitchen paper, reserving the rest of the oil.

Put the fried onions, chopped onion, yogurt, mustard oil, remaining 1 tbsp vegetable oil, almonds, chillies, coriander, roast and ground cumin and fennel seeds, garam masala and some salt into a food processor and blend to a very smooth paste.

Remove the marinated beef from the fridge and uncover. Pour the blended second marinade on to the beef and combine thoroughly. Cover and refrigerate for a further two to four hours. Meanwhile, soak a handful of bamboo skewers in warm water.

When the beef is ready to cook, bring it to room temperature. Skewer all the pieces gently through the middle with the bamboo skewers and cook – either under a hot grill or on a barbecue – basting regularly with the reserved oil to brown the meat evenly. Two minutes on each side will be enough for rare meat.

SERVES 4–6

Serve with **Sambal with Lemon Grass** *(see page 139),* and **Broad Bean Quinoa** *(see page 130)*

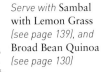

Lamb and potato korma

A simple but gorgeous dish with a great creaminess from the nuts and seeds. The potatoes need to be cooked until they are really soft. You will probably want to have some vibrant green beans with this, to counteract the richness.

2 tsp blanched almonds
1 tsp coriander seeds
2 tsp sesame seeds
2 tsp white poppy seeds
2 tsp cumin seeds
500g lamb, cut into 2.5cm cubes
1½ tsp crushed garlic
1½ tsp grated root ginger
½ tsp turmeric
1 tsp chilli powder
salt
125ml vegetable oil
4 green cardamom pods
4 cloves
4 x 5cm cinnamon sticks
450g onions, thinly sliced
125g yogurt
350g potatoes, quartered
100ml coconut milk
2 tbsp chopped coriander leaves

Place the almonds and the coriander, sesame, poppy and cumin seeds into a dry frying pan. Toast over a medium heat, stirring, until slightly darker and aromatic. Remove from the pan and grind them together in a coffee or spice grinder until very fine. Set aside.

Put the meat into a bowl with the garlic, ginger, turmeric, chilli and salt to taste. Mix well, cover and leave to marinate in the fridge for one hour.

Heat the oil until hot in a saucepan and add the cardamom, cloves and cinnamon and allow to sizzle for a few seconds, then add the onions. Fry until golden brown. Add the marinated meat and stir-fry for five minutes, until browned all over.

Mix together the ground roasted spice mixture with the yogurt and pour the mixture on to the meat. Stir-fry for another five minutes, then add 300ml of water and bring to the boil. Reduce the heat and simmer for about 25 minutes, then add the potatoes. Continue to simmer for about 20 minutes, until the meat is tender and the potatoes are cooked.

Add the coconut milk, cover and cook over a low heat until the oil separates, adding a little water if necessary; the sauce should be thick. Remove the whole spices, if you prefer, and serve, sprinkled with the chopped coriander.

SERVES 4–6

Serve with Coconut Rice *(see page 132), and* French Beans with Sesame Seeds *(see page 118)*

Lamb pasanda with green mangoes

A lovely summer dish. A sweetness comes through from the mangoes, while the ginger in the recipe helps to keep the body cool in hot weather. 'Pasanda' simply means flattened meat. People think the word refers to the sauce, and that anything called pasanda will be rich and creamy, but in fact a pasanda can have any type of sauce.

500g lean lamb fillet, cut into 5cm pieces
4–5 tbsp ghee or oil
4 x 5cm cinnamon sticks
4 green cardamom pods
2 black cardamom pods
2 small onions, thinly sliced
1½ tbsp grated root ginger
salt
1½ tbsp ground coriander
½ tsp garam masala
500g unripe green mangoes, peeled, cut into 2.5cm-thick long slices
200g caster sugar
½ tsp ground mace

Place the pieces of lamb between sheets of cling film and beat it flat with a rolling pin.

Heat the ghee in a wide, heavy-based pan until it begins to smoke. Add the cinnamon and both types of cardamom pods and allow the spices to splutter. Immediately add the onions and fry until they turn golden brown. Add the ginger and cook for a minute or two.

Now add the lamb and brown on all sides, then add salt to taste and the ground coriander. Cook for two to three minutes, stirring; the onion mixture should coat the meat. Pour in about 230ml of water. Bring to the boil, then reduce the heat, cover and simmer until the meat is tender and the sauce fairly thick (about 15–20 minutes). Add the garam masala and simmer for a further minute.

Meanwhile, bring just enough water to the boil in a separate saucepan to cover the mango slices. Prod each slice with a fork to pierce it, and add to the water. Boil for five to 10 minutes, until half-cooked. Remove and drain. Put the sugar and 100ml of water in another saucepan and cook over a low heat to a thick syrup. Add the mangoes and the mace. Simmer until the syrup has almost evaporated. Add the mangoes to the meat, with a little water, and simmer until the ghee separates and films on the surface. Serve.

SERVES 4

Serve with **Spinach and Leek Rice** *(see page 133)*

Tandoori lamb racks

Get the butcher to French-trim the racks of lamb. They must also be trimmed of all their fat. I often use two marinades in my cooking: the first is to break down the fibres and remove the moisture from the meat; the second to return the moisture and also to infiltrate the meat with flavour and juiciness.

FOR THE FIRST MARINADE
3 tsp grated root ginger
2 tsp crushed garlic
1–2 tsp freshly ground
black pepper
1–2 tsp garam masala
2–3 green chillies,
finely chopped
juice of 1 lemon
1 tsp salt

FOR THE LAMB
2 French-trimmed racks of
lamb, each about 8 bones, each
rack weighing 350g after being
trimmed of all their fat

FOR THE SECOND MARINADE
165g soft cream cheese
100g cheddar cheese,
finely grated
100g mozzarella cheese,
finely grated
150ml single cream

Mix all the ingredients for the first marinade in a large bowl, add the racks and mix thoroughly. Cover and leave to marinate in the fridge for at least two hours.

In a separate bowl, combine the ingredients for the second marinade and whisk lightly. Pour this mixture into the marinated lamb, cover and refrigerate overnight.

When you are ready to cook, return the racks to room temperature and preheat the oven to 200°C/400°F/gas mark 6. Cook the lamb racks for 25–30 minutes for medium meat, which is pink in the centre. Serve.

SERVES 4–6

Serve with **Broad Bean Quinoa** *(see page 130),* *and* **Shredded Green Mango Pickle** *(see page 139)*

New-style bunny chow

'Bunny chow' is a traditional dish in South Africa; it was created by Indian immigrants. Under the apartheid regime, excluded people were not allowed to be served food. To get around this, enterprising restaurant owners used to hollow out a loaf of bread, fill it with bunny chow, and pass it through a hatch. When I was in Durban, I was asked to make my version of bunny chow, and this is it. I thought this recipe for lamb in pickling spices combined with brioche would be ideal, as the slight bitterness of the spices lends itself rather marvellously to the sweet bread. This curry is a very good-tempered dish, it can be made in advance and also freezes well; the flavours will deepen.

500g lean lamb cut into 5cm cubes
salt
1 tsp turmeric
25ml mustard oil (optional)
100g ghee or vegetable oil
4 onions, thinly sliced
4–6 dried red chillies
6 cloves
3 black cardamom pods
4 green cardamom pods
1 tsp black mustard seeds
1 tsp cumin seeds
½ tsp fennel seeds
½ tsp nigella seeds
¼ tsp fenugreek seeds
pinch of asafoetida
4–6 garlic cloves, crushed
5cm piece of root ginger, grated
1 tsp chilli powder
1–2 tbsp gur (sugar molasses, optional)
juice of 1 lime
4 brioche buns, to serve

Put the meat into a saucepan with a tight-fitting lid. Pour in just enough water to cover. Bring to the boil, skim any scum from the surface, then add salt to taste and the turmeric. Cover, reduce the heat, then simmer until most of the liquid has been absorbed and the meat is tender; this will take 45 minutes to one hour. Remove the meat with a slotted spoon, reserving any remaining liquid.

In a separate pan, heat the mustard oil, if using, with the ghee or oil. Once the oil begins to smoke, add the onions and fry until golden brown, then remove with a slotted spoon and drain on kitchen paper. Add the whole dried chillies to the remaining oil in the pan and fry until they blacken, then remove the pan from the heat and discard the chillies. Return the oil to the heat once again, then add the cloves and both types of cardamom pods, allowing them to sizzle for a few seconds. Now add the mustard, cumin, fennel, nigella and fenugreek seeds and the asafoetida. Once the seeds begin to crackle and pop, add the garlic and ginger. Stir-fry for a minute, then add the cooked meat with the chilli powder and sugar molasses, if using. Stir-fry for a further few minutes, adding the leftover meat stock, if there is any.

Add the lime juice with 2 tbsp water and simmer over a low heat until all the moisture has evaporated and only the ghee remains on top.

Serve in a hollowed out brioche bun, sprinkled with the fried onions. Or, if you prefer, leave out the brioche buns and serve with chapatis.

SERVES 4

Serve with French Beans with Sesame Seeds *(see page 118)*

Laal maas

This means 'red meat'. It is a fiery Rajasthani dish, and famous in that state. There are a lot of chillies here, but trust me. My version is hot, but not aggressively so, and the yogurt mellows it out, so I promise it won't send you into another orbit. Serve it with raita, in case you need a bit of cooling down...

FOR THE LAMB
15 dried red chillies, stalks removed, broken into 2–3 pieces
2 tbsp tomato purée
3 tbsp ghee or vegetable oil
6–8 cloves
6 green cardamom pods
3 black cardamom pods
2 bay leaves
2 large onions, thinly sliced
8 garlic cloves, crushed
3 tbsp grated root ginger
1kg lamb, cut into 4cm cubes, preferably with bones in
550ml lamb stock or water
juice of 1 lemon
2 tbsp chopped coriander leaves

FOR THE YOGURT MIXTURE
1½ tsp cumin seeds
225g yogurt, lightly whisked
2½ tsp ground coriander
2 tsp chilli powder
salt

FOR TEMPERING
2 tbsp ghee or vegetable oil

Soak all the dried red chillies in warm water for 30 minutes, then drain and set aside six to eight of them for the tempering. Put the tomato purée in a small cup and dilute with 2 tbsp water. Set aside.

Place the cumin seeds for the yogurt mixture in a small dry frying pan over a medium heat. Stir until they turn a shade darker and smell aromatic. Tip into a bowl with all the other ingredients for the yogurt mixture, mix together and set aside.

For the lamb, in a large heavy-based pan, heat the ghee or oil over a medium-high heat until hot. Add the cloves, green and black cardamom pods, bay leaves and four of the soaked dried chillies. Once they begin to crackle and change colour, add the onions, garlic and ginger. Continue to sauté until the mixture turns a pale almond brown. Now add the meat and cook, stirring continuously, over a high heat for about five minutes, then add the rest of the soaked dried chillies. Continue to cook for a further 10 minutes or so, or until all the liquid has evaporated and the meat starts to brown. Reduce the heat to medium, then add the yogurt mixture. Cook for a further 15 minutes, or until the yogurt has been absorbed. Pour in the stock and the tomato purée mixture. Bring to the boil, cover and simmer for 30–40 minutes, until tender. Once the meat is done, remove from the heat and keep warm.

Using a small frying pan, heat the ghee or oil for tempering until very hot, add the reserved dried chillies and, as soon they change colour, pour on to the lamb.

Finally, add the lemon juice and the chopped coriander, taste and adjust the seasoning, and serve.

SERVES 4–6

Serve with **Perfect Rice** *(see page 132), and* **Cucumber Raita** *(see page 139)*

Perfect
PARTNERS

Mooli and pomegranate salad

This is colourful, jewel-like and ravishing both to look at and to eat. I think of it as a Silk Route salad, in which sharp Middle Eastern pomegranate meets vibrant Indian mint and hot radish. Quite crunchy and peppery, its freshness works really well with grilled meats – such as chicken tikka or any tandoori dish – and is also fabulous with fish. Very versatile and refreshing, this salad is a welcome addition to almost any Indian-inspired meal.

FOR THE SALAD
400g mooli or daikon), peeled and julienned (see page 125)
1–2 carrots, peeled and julienned
seeds of 2 pomegranates
120g flaked almonds, toasted
leaves from a few sprigs of mint and coriander

FOR THE DRESSING
2 tbsp lime juice
1 tbsp toasted sesame oil
1 tsp salt
½ tsp chilli powder
2 tsp caster sugar or honey

Soak the julienned mooli in iced water for 15 minutes, then rinse, drain and pat dry with kitchen paper.

Place the mooli, carrots, pomegranate seeds and almonds in a serving bowl.

For the dressing, thoroughly mix all the ingredients and adjust the seasoning to taste. Pour over the salad, toss well, cover and chill for 30 minutes. Fold in the herb leaves just before serving.

SERVES 4–6 AS A SIDE DISH

Serve with **Beef Satay** *(see page 25)*

Beetroot and radish salad

I am a huge fan of beetroot and find it hard to believe that other people don't feel the same about these sweet, unbelievably coloured spheres... Probably those who are wary of beetroot had the same upbringing as myself, with overexposure to soggy, sour beetroot in vinegar. But those days are over! The earthy flavours here are delicious with the peppery radishes. The dressing is very subtle, but it complements any spicy dish. If you don't like raw onions, souse them first in lemon juice and salt for about 10 minutes to remove their bitterness.

FOR THE DRESSING
150ml rapeseed oil
1 lemon grass stalk
1 tsp black mustard seeds
finely grated zest of 1 lime and juice of 2
1–2 tbsp caster sugar or honey

FOR THE SALAD
850g raw beetroots
salt
freshly ground black pepper
100g radishes, thinly sliced
1 small red onion, thinly sliced
2 tbsp snipped chives
2 tbsp roughly chopped mint leaves
2 tbsp roughly chopped coriander leaves

Heat the oil in a pan over a gentle heat. Smash up the lemon grass stalk and add it to the oil to infuse for just a few minutes. Remove from the heat and set aside for a few hours to intensify the flavour. (This can be done well in advance and it is nice to do extra quantities to keep in the larder; it is a useful dressing to have to hand.)

Preheat the oven to 200°C/400°F/gas mark 6. Wash and scrub the beetroots. Place each on a piece of foil, drizzle with a little of the infused oil and season lightly. Wrap them in the foil and place on a baking tray. Cook in the oven for one hour, or until tender. Allow to cool for 20 minutes. Peel the beetroots, cut into wedges and place in a bowl. Add all the remaining salad ingredients.

To make the dressing, reheat the remaining lemon grass-infused oil in a frying pan. Add the mustard seeds and allow to pop. This will take a few seconds. Allow the oil to cool. Add the lime zest and juice and the sugar or honey and mix well, until the sugar dissolves. Toss the dressing over the salad and serve.

SERVES 4 AS A SIDE DISH

Kachumbar

This word simply means 'cucumber'. It is a lovely relish which is extremely versatile and goes with everything. For a photo, see page 36.

2 large tomatoes, diced
1 cucumber, diced
1 large red onion, finely diced
½ tsp chaat masala
juice of 1 lime
salt

Mix all the ingredients together in a bowl and season with salt to taste.

SERVES 4 AS A SIDE DISH

Serve Kachumbar with Spicy Stuffed Potatoes (see page 37), or Beetroot and Radish Salad with Chilli-seared Mackerel (see page 20)

Roast potatoes with chilli and chaat masala

There's nothing better than delicious roast potatoes, especially when enhanced by a kick of chilli and spicy chaat masala. This dish works a dream with roast guinea fowl, duck breasts or sweet and sour chicken. You can use exactly the same method for roast parsnips. Simply par-boil the parsnips, then tip immediately into the hot oil and spices, adding a sprinkle of brown sugar or a drizzle of honey. For a photo of the potatoes, see page 39.

1kg potatoes (Maris Piper or King Edward are best for this)
salt
vegetable oil or ghee
3 garlic cloves, crushed
1 tsp chilli flakes
2 tsp chaat masala

Preheat the oven to 200°C/400°F/gas mark 6. Peel the potatoes and cut them in half lengthways. Place them into a saucepan and cover with cold salted water. Bring to the boil and simmer for six to seven minutes. Drain in a colander and allow to stand for a few minutes before shaking them gently; you want to break down the edges of the potatoes to get them to go crisp during the roasting process.

In the meantime, heat a roasting tray with a 5mm layer of oil or ghee in the oven and toss the potatoes with the garlic, chilli flakes and half the chaat masala. Roast for up to an hour, until golden and crispy, turning occasionally. Remove from the oven, sprinkle with the remaining chaat masala, and serve.

SERVES 4 AS A SIDE DISH

Potatoes and peas with fenugreek

Fenugreek has a very distinct flavour. The leaves are used as a herb and the seeds as a spice. The leaves can be fresh or dried and they are very bitter. If you use fresh leaves, you should blanch them first, to remove some of that bitterness. Dried fenugreek is quite strong. Both intensify sauces beautifully.

1–2 tbsp vegetable oil
1 tsp cumin seeds
1 green chilli, finely chopped
1 large potato, in 5mm dice
salt
¼ tsp turmeric
75g frozen peas
1 tsp crushed dried fenugreek
1 tbsp toasted sesame seeds
1 tbsp chopped coriander leaves

Heat the oil in a frying pan which has a lid over a medium-high heat and add the cumin seeds. Once they crackle, add the chilli and stir-fry for a few seconds. Add the potato, salt and turmeric. Sprinkle over 4 tbsp of water, cover, and steam for three to four minutes, until just cooked. Uncover and stir in the peas and fenugreek. Cook until heated through with no remaining liquid. Toss in the sesame seeds and coriander, then serve.

SERVES 2–3 AS A SIDE DISH

Serve with **Sweet and Sour Stuffed Chicken** *(see page 38)*

Beansprout salad with chargrilled asparagus and coconut

This lovely, refreshing salad works well with very many dishes, especially tandoori preparations and any grilled meats; lamb chops would be great, as the salad will cut through their richness. There are a lovely combination of textures here, embracing both North and South with the European asparagus and Indian coconut. The salad looks beautifully verdant and spring-like, and is a lovely way to celebrate the arrival of the first asparagus spears, peeping through the soil. It is also wonderful as a palate cleanser, welcome after any rich meal.

100g broad beans, podded
200g beansprouts
200g asparagus spears
2–3 tbsp vegetable oil
1 tsp black mustard seeds
1 tsp cumin seeds
1–2 sprigs of curry leaves
½ tsp crushed garlic
½ tsp grated root ginger
1–2 green chillies, deseeded and finely chopped
salt
100g freshly grated or shaved coconut
50g pomegranate seeds
handful of coriander leaves
2 tsp caster sugar, or to taste
juice of 2 limes, or to taste

If using frozen broad beans, put them in a bowl, cover with water and leave to soak while you prepare the other ingredients, then slip off the skins.

If using fresh broad beans, bring a saucepan of water to the boil and blanch the beans for two to three minutes. Refresh in cold water and slip off the skins.

Rinse the beansprouts in cold water. Drop them in boiling water and allow to stand for a minute. Drain thoroughly, then refresh in very cold water to stop the cooking. Set aside.

Preheat a griddle pan on a medium-high heat. Brush the asparagus with a little oil and place them on the griddle pan in a single layer. (You may have to work in batches.) Cook for two to three minutes, turning occasionally, until tender but still crisp and lightly browned. Set aside.

Heat the remaining oil in a frying pan until hot. Add the mustard and cumin seeds. Once they begin to pop and splutter, add the curry leaves, garlic and ginger. Cook for a minute or so, then add the drained broad beans with the chillies. Add some salt with a dash of water to allow the beans to cook until just tender. When all the liquid has been absorbed, remove from the heat and set aside.

In a large mixing bowl, toss together the beansprouts, asparagus, broad bean mixture and the rest of the ingredients. Adjust the seasoning with more salt, sugar or lime juice, to taste.

SERVES 4 AS A SIDE DISH

Serve with Tandoori King Prawns *(see page 87)*

French beans with sesame seeds

You must try this dish. For those who don't like their greens, this is one that will convert you. It is a fantastic accompaniment to a roast dinner, but so versatile that it will go with a pulao, a biryani or the Baked Baby Aubergines (see page 57) as a showing off dish. Make sure the water for blanching the beans is really well salted; it will turn them bright green and get rid of any impurities, and is all washed off anyway in the iced water bath. The lime and sugar sends it to a different level, while the spices have that wonderful south Indian influence. For a photo, see page 108.

400g French beans
salt
2–3 tbsp vegetable oil
generous pinch of asafoetida
1 tsp black mustard seeds
1 tsp cumin seeds
½ tsp fennel seeds
2 sprigs of curry leaves
1 onion, finely chopped
1 tsp crushed garlic
1 tsp grated root ginger
1 fresh red chilli, deseeded if you like, finely chopped
1–2 tsp caster sugar
juice of 1 lime
1 tbsp toasted sesame seeds
1 tbsp chopped coriander

Top and tail the beans, de-string and cut into 2.5cm lengths if necessary, depending on the size and age of the beans. Blanch in boiling salted water for three or four minutes. Drain, and immediately plunge the beans into cold water to prevent further cooking. When cold, drain well and pat dry with kitchen paper.

Pour 2 tbsp of oil into a non-stick frying pan or wok and place on a high heat. As soon as it starts to smoke, add the asafoetida, mustard, cumin and fennel seeds as well as the curry leaves. As soon as they begin to pop and splutter, add the onion, garlic and ginger. Cook until the onion is soft and beginning to brown at the edges. Now add the chilli and stir-fry for a few seconds, before adding the drained beans. Heat through, continuing to stir.

Finally add the sugar, lime juice, toasted sesame seeds and the chopped coriander, taste, and add more salt if you think it needs it. Serve immediately.

SERVES 4–6 AS A SIDE DISH

Serve with **New-style Bunny Chow** *(see page 107)*

Stuffed baked aubergines

Aubergines just lend themselves to a good stuffing! I make no apology at all for including two stuffed aubergine recipes in this book; they are stupendously delicious. This recipe uses a large aubergine, the slices stuffed in the centre. The filling can be made the day before. It makes an excellent starter on its own or, for a celebratory vegetarian spread, serve with Panchrattan Dal (see page 34), and rice or any Indian breads.

FOR THE STUFFING
100g boiled potatoes, grated
100g grated paneer or crumbled ricotta cheese
2 tsp toasted sesame seeds
1 tsp chopped green chilli
1 tsp chilli powder
salt

FOR THE SAUCE
40ml sunflower or vegetable oil
1 tsp black mustard seeds
1 sprig of curry leaves
1 tsp chopped green chilli
1 tsp chilli powder
pinch of asafoetida
200g chopped canned tomatoes
2 tsp caster sugar

FOR THE AUBERGINE ROUNDS
1 large aubergine
1 tsp chilli powder
plain flour, to dust
vegetable oil, to shallow-fry
2 tbsp chopped coriander leaves

First, make the stuffing. Mix together all the ingredients in a mixing bowl, adding salt to taste.

Now to make the sauce. Heat the oil in a heavy-based saucepan until hot and add the mustard seeds. Just as they begin to pop and crackle, add the curry leaves, green chilli, chilli powder, asafoetida, tomatoes, sugar and salt to taste. Bring to the boil, reduce the heat and simmer to reduce the sauce to a thick consistency.

Cut the aubergine into 2cm rounds and, with a sharp knife, remove and discard the pulp in the centre, forming a hollow ring. Toss the aubergine rings with some salt and the chilli powder and set aside in a colander for about 20 minutes, while you preheat the oven to 180°C/350°F/gas mark 4.

Stuff the aubergine rings tightly with the stuffing mixture, then dust evenly with the flour. Shallow-fry on both sides in the hot oil until they form a golden crust.

Place the stuffed aubergine slices on a baking tray and top with the sauce. Bake in the hot oven for 10–20 minutes, until cooked and heated through.

Serve sprinkled with the coriander, with a dollop of yogurt mixed with garlic and mint, and topped with ginger julienne, if you want to be posh about it!

SERVES 3 AS A STARTER OR 4 AS A SIDE DISH

Serve with Fried Plantains with Yogurt Sauce *(see page 127), or* Sweet-sour Lamb Pulao *(see page 51)*

Celeriac gratin with cinnamon and onion confit

This is a great vegetable speciality for the winter months. The sweetness of the onions and cinnamon brings out the lovely flavour of the celeriac. The onions need to cook on a very low heat until the sweetness comes through and they become very soft and almost melt. In my opinion, celeriac is not used as much as it should be, it's a very healthy root. Don't be put off: when you see it, it may look like a hairy mine, but inside you will find a beautiful white purity of flesh. If you slice celeriac ahead of time, you will have to put it in a bowl of acidulated water to stop it from discolouring. For a photo of the finished dish, see page 70.

1kg celeriac, peeled and thinly sliced
6 tbsp olive oil
4 onions, thinly sliced
3 garlic cloves, crushed
25g unsalted butter
salt
1 tsp chilli flakes
1 tsp ground cinnamon
150ml double cream
150ml whole milk

Preheat the oven to 180°C/350°F/gas mark 4. Wash the celeriac slices to remove any excess starch, then dry thoroughly.

Heat the oil in a wide sauté pan and add the onions and garlic. Cook over a low heat until they become soft and sweet; this will take about 30 minutes. Remove with a slotted spoon and drain off any excess oil.

Butter a gratin dish and arrange a layer of the celeriac slices over it. Sprinkle over some of the onion confit with some salt, chilli flakes and cinnamon, then continue to layer until you have used them all up.

Mix together the cream and milk and pour over the celeriac. Cover with foil and place in the hot oven. Cook for about 1 hour 15 minutes, until tender to the point of a knife. Remove the foil 10 minutes before the end of cooking to allow the top to brown.

SERVES 4–6 AS A SIDE DISH

Serve with Duck Breasts with Orange, Ginger and Cinnamon *(see page 71)*

Spiced vegetable polenta

A great vegetarian dish. On my travels in Rajasthan, I met with a desert tribe, the Bishnoi, and they used a lot of millet and cornmeal in their cooking. Because of the limitations of their environment, dried pulses and grains are the staple of their diet. Cornmeal is very similar to polenta, so this recipe was inspired by what the desert tribe was eating. You can use any mixed vegetables, whatever you like or have in the cupboard.

200g polenta
2–3 tbsp vegetable oil
pinch of asafoetida
1 tsp cumin seeds
4–6 tbsp tomato purée
400g cooked mixed vegetables
(shelled broad beans, carrots, small broccoli florets)
1 heaped tsp dried fenugreek leaves
½ red onion, finely chopped
salt
juice of ½ lemon
pinch of caster sugar
2 tbsp ghee or vegetable oil
2.5cm piece of root ginger, cut into julienne
2 green chillies, deseeded if you like, finely chopped
1 tbsp roughly chopped coriander leaves

Bring 800ml of water to the boil in a saucepan. Add the polenta and whisk furiously for one to two minutes until the polenta swells and soaks up all the liquid. (Whisking stops it getting lumpy.)

Next, heat the oil in a separate pan until hot and add the asafoetida and cumin seeds. Now add the tomato purée and some water to loosen the mixture and create a sauce-like consistency. Add the cooked vegetables with the fenugreek leaves, red onion and salt to taste. Allow this mixture to cook for a few minutes, or until the vegetables have warmed through. Remove from the heat and stir in the lemon juice and sugar.

Finish the polenta by adding the ghee or oil and stirring well. Loosen with a little warm water to get a smooth consistency.

Serve by spooning the polenta into a warmed dish and topping with the vegetable mixture. Sprinkle with the ginger julienne, chillies and roughly chopped coriander.

SERVES 4 AS A MAIN COURSE

Serve with Tomato and Ginger Chutney *(see page 22)*

Beetroot pachadi

These flavours are typically south Indian, where they always use both yogurt and coconut. Beetroot is a very western ingredient and I love it both for its vibrant colour and wonderfully earthy taste.

100g freshly grated coconut, or 50g desiccated coconut soaked in warm water for a few minutes and squeezed dry
2 green chillies
2.5cm piece of root ginger, finely chopped
4 large raw beetroot
2 tbsp vegetable oil
1½ tsp black mustard seeds
10–15 curry leaves
1 tsp chilli powder
½ tsp turmeric
salt
225g yogurt

Put the coconut, chillies and ginger in a blender, adding a dash of water. Blitz until very smooth. Set aside. Cut the beetroot into wedges or cubes. Bring a saucepan of water to the boil and add the beetroot. Cook for 20 minutes, or until tender. Drain and set aside.

Heat the oil in a large frying pan or wok over a medium-high heat until hot. Add the mustard seeds and, as they begin to pop, add the curry leaves. Add the beetroot, chilli powder and turmeric with salt to taste. Cook for two minutes over a medium heat, stirring frequently. Now add the coconut mixture and cook over a low heat for about five minutes, stirring from time to time. If the mixture starts to stick, add a dash of water to stop it burning. Remove from the heat, season the yogurt with salt, then loosely fold it in and serve.

SERVES 4 AS A SIDE DISH

Saffron-roast cauliflower

Roasting cauliflower brings out a lovely colour and flavour, so if you've never tried it, you really should. The saffron is marvellous in this Indo-Middle Eastern recipe.

1½ tsp saffron threads
1 cauliflower, cut into florets
1 large red onion, thinly sliced
1 tsp grated root ginger
4 tbsp vegetable oil
2 bay leaves
½ tsp chilli flakes
½ tsp roughly crushed cumin seeds
salt

TO SERVE
1 tsp vegetable oil or butter
2 tbsp pine nuts
3 tbsp raisins, soaked in water, then squeezed dry
4 tbsp chopped coriander leaves

Soak the saffron in 75ml boiling water for five minutes. Preheat the oven to 200°C/400°F/gas mark 6.

Mix all the ingredients thoroughly in a bowl. Transfer to an ovenproof dish and cover with foil. Bake in the oven for 40–45 minutes. Halfway through cooking, remove the dish from the oven and stir well. Uncover and return to the oven to allow the cauliflower to cook until just tender and browned. Remove the dish from the oven once the cauliflower is done and allow to cool slightly.

Meanwhile, heat the oil or butter in a frying pan and sauté the pine nuts until they turn a pale golden colour, then add the raisins and stir-fry for a few seconds. Once the raisins begin to puff up, toss the mixture over the cauliflower. Stir in the coriander. Adjust the seasoning and serve warm or at room temperature.

SERVES 4 AS A SIDE DISH

Kidney beans with dried lime

This may look murky, but don't worry about that; the flavours are deeply fabulous with a lovely herbaceous taste to the sauce. Sprinkle the finished dish with more herbs if the look of it bothers you. This is a great recipe for vegetarians on its own; serve with a dollop of yogurt flavoured with ground roasted cumin and roasted garlic, and some plain rice. For a photo, see page 40.

6 tbsp vegetable oil or ghee
good pinch of asafoetida
1 tsp cumin seeds
1 large onion, thinly sliced
4 garlic cloves, crushed
2 green chillies, finely chopped
140g flat leaf parsley, finely chopped
140g leeks, finely chopped
80g coriander leaves, finely chopped
80g fresh fenugreek leaves, chopped, or 3 tbsp dried fenugreek leaves
1½ tsp salt
freshly ground black pepper
½ tsp turmeric
1 tsp dried lime powder (optional)
2 x 400g cans kidney beans, drained and rinsed
4 tbsp fresh lime juice

Heat the oil or ghee in a wide saucepan over a medium heat until very hot. Add the asafoetida, followed by the cumin seeds. Allow the seeds to splutter for a few seconds, then add the onion. Sauté for six to eight minutes, until the onion becomes really soft and translucent. Now add the garlic, chillies, parsley, leeks, coriander and fenugreek and fry for a good eight to 10 minutes, stirring occasionally. This will bring out the flavour of the aromatics. Add the salt, pepper to taste, turmeric and lime powder, if using. Stir-fry for two minutes.

Pour in 650ml of water and bring to the boil. Reduce the heat to low, cover and simmer for 20 minutes, stirring occasionally. Stir in the beans. Add the lime juice, cover partially and simmer over a medium-low heat, stirring occasionally, until the beans are piping hot. Adjust the seasoning and serve.

SERVES 4–6 AS A SIDE DISH

Serve with **Persian Chicken with Saffron and Cardamom** *(see page 41)*

Gingered carrots with maple syrup

Glazed carrots are a classic idea, but this recipe is enhanced by Indian flavours. Jewel-like in colour, the carrots bring a vibrancy to any table, while their natural sweetness will complement many dishes. As an alternative to maple syrup you could use agave nectar, or add toasted pumpkin seeds for a bit of crunch, if you like. In this recipe, the carrots are cut into julienne, which is a posh name for matchsticks. It's easier to do this if you first cut the carrots into 7.5cm lengths, slice them, then stack the slices and slice again, this time into thin, 6mm strips.

FOR THE CARROTS
4 tbsp unsalted butter
1 tbsp grated root ginger
450g carrots, in large julienne
(about 7.5cm x 6mm x 6mm)
½ tsp chilli flakes
2 tbsp maple syrup
salt
1 tbsp chopped coriander leaves

FOR THE TEMPERING
1 tbsp rapeseed or vegetable oil
1 tsp black mustard seeds
1 tsp cumin seeds

Melt half the butter in a large, deep frying pan over a medium heat. Add the ginger, carrots, chilli flakes and syrup. Stir and cook for one to two minutes. Add water so that the carrots are just covered and bring to the boil over a high heat. Cover with a lid and cook for about five minutes, until the carrots turn a bright orange. Make sure you don't add too much water, or the carrots might overcook. Remove the lid and continue to cook over a medium-high heat until all the water has evaporated and the carrots have begun to caramelise in the maple syrup.

In a separate pan, heat the oil for tempering until it begins to smoke. Add the mustard and cumin seeds. Once they begin to pop and splutter, toss immediately on to the carrots. Adjust the seasoning and sprinkle with the chopped coriander.

SERVES 4 AS A SIDE DISH

Serve with **Paupiettes of Lemon Sole with Saffron Sauce** *(see page 59)*

Fried plantains in a yogurt sauce

A south Indian dish, this would go very well with spicy, rich meat recipes. This can be served as a posh canapé, as in the photo, with the yogurt sauce used as a dip and a pile of cocktail sticks for skewering the plantains, or you can just mix the plantains and sauce together and serve with rice; so it's a two-in-one dish!

4 tbsp raisins
2 tsp cumin seeds
vegetable oil, to deep-fry, plus a little more
4 tbsp pine nuts
6 large, ripe plantains
35g fresh coconut, grated
3 red chillies
6 garlic cloves
1–2 tbsp chopped coriander leaves
1–2 tbsp chopped mint leaves, plus more to serve (optional)
500g Greek-style yogurt
salt
3 tbsp caster sugar

Soak the raisins in hot water for 15 minutes, then drain. Place the cumin seeds in a dry frying pan placed over a medium heat and stir until they are aromatic. Set aside.

Heat a little oil in the same frying pan and add the pine nuts. Cook, stirring, until the pine nuts are golden. Add the raisins and stir for a few seconds until plump, hot and juicy. Set aside.

Peel the plantains and cut each into thin slices. Heat the oil for deep-frying over a medium heat in a wok or a deep fat-fryer, until it reaches 180°C (350°F). Fry the plantains in batches until they caramelise and form a crust. Remove with a slotted spoon and leave to drain on kitchen paper.

Put the coconut, chillies, cumin, garlic and herbs in a blender and blitz to a very fine paste with a splash of water. Whisk the yogurt lightly and add salt to taste and the sugar. Mix in the blended coconut mixture. Add the raisins and pine nuts, reserving a little of each.

To serve, pour some of the yogurt into a serving bowl, add the plantains and pour more of the yogurt over the top. Sprinkle with the sautéed nuts and raisins. Serve cold. Alternatively, serve the yogurt sauce in a bowl, sprinkled with a few mint leaves, and offer the plantain slices alongside.

SERVES 4–6 AS A SIDE DISH

Serve with **Khichri** *(see page 129)*

Colourful spiced cabbage

An easy winner. This is a very versatile side dish: clean, fresh, colourful, fragrant and spicy. It would be a lovely contrast to any main dish that is rich and creamy, as the cabbage remains crunchy. It's a great way of eating this humble veg, which is so looked down upon, despite being so high in nutrients. The colours are wonderful, with the orange and red of the carrots and tomatoes. For a photo, see page 96.

4 tbsp vegetable oil
½ tsp black mustard seeds
1 tsp cumin seeds
2 onions, finely chopped
¼ tsp turmeric
1 green chilli, finely chopped
½ tsp chilli powder
2cm piece of root ginger, grated
200g carrots, cut into julienne
300g Savoy cabbage, shredded
2 tomatoes, deseeded, finely chopped and lightly salted
salt
caster sugar
2 tbsp chopped coriander leaves

Heat the oil in a wok over a medium-high heat until hot, add both the mustard and cumin seeds and allow to crackle. Add the onions, turmeric and green chilli. Cook the onions until soft and about to change colour.

Now add the chilli powder and ginger and stir for a few more seconds. Add the carrots and continue to cook for a couple of minutes so they start to sweat and soften, then add the cabbage.

Stir-fry for a few minutes, then reduce the heat and add the tomatoes, with salt and sugar to taste. Cook to your preferred consistency, finally adding the coriander to serve.

SERVES 4 AS A SIDE DISH

Serve with Spinach and Apricot Stuffed Chicken with Korma Sauce *(see page 97)*

Spinach with radish greens

The bitterness here is brilliant with any dish that is slightly sweet or rich, as it cuts through those flavours. If you come across radishes with greens, then snap them up, the leaves will be slightly bitter. If you can't find them, you can replace them with kale or even chard. For a photo, see page 92.

60g vegetable oil
1 tsp cumin seeds
1 tsp fennel seeds
3 hot dried red chillies
2 onions, finely sliced
900g spinach, roughly chopped
225g radish greens, stems removed, roughly chopped
salt
15g unsalted butter

Heat the oil in a wide pan until hot. Add the cumin and fennel seeds and the chillies. Once the spices begin to crackle and the chillies turn a shade darker, add the onions. Stir-fry for seven to eight minutes, until the onions turn soft and translucent.

Add the spinach, radish greens and some salt. Continue to cook and stir until all the liquid evaporates; it will take about 15 minutes. Cover and cook over a very low heat for a further five minutes. Stir in the butter until it melts and makes the leaves glossy, then serve.

SERVES 4–6 AS A SIDE DISH

Khichri

A preparation of rice and lentils and an Indian comfort food; the British dish kedgeree came from this. There's nothing better than khichri if you're feeling delicate. It's fabulous with dry spiced fish dishes and yogurt dip.

2 tbsp ghee or oil
2 bay leaves
3 black cardamom pods
1 tsp cumin seeds
2 x 5cm cinnamon sticks or cassia bark
3 cloves
2 onions, finely sliced
salt
3 garlic cloves, crushed
2.5cm root ginger, grated
150g moong dal, washed, soaked in water for 30 minutes
½ tsp turmeric
400g basmati rice, washed, soaked in water for 30 minutes

Heat a heavy-based pan until hot. Add the ghee, bay leaves, black cardamom, cumin, cinnamon sticks and cloves. Allow to crackle for a few seconds, then add the onions. Fry, stirring occasionally, until the onions turn pale brown around the edges. Add a pinch of salt, the garlic and ginger, and stir well. Drain the lentils and add to the pan with the turmeric and about 50ml water. Reduce the heat, cover and simmer for about 10 minutes, stirring from time to time, until the lentils soften. If it becomes too dry, add a little more water.

Drain the rice and add to the lentils with about 850ml hot water and 2 tsp salt. Bring to the boil and cook until most of the liquid has evaporated and small craters form on the surface. Reduce the heat to a minimum, cover with a dry cloth and a tight-fitting lid. Leave for 15 minutes, until all the moisture has been absorbed, then serve.

SERVES 4 AS A SIDE DISH

Serve **Khichri** *with chilli-seared Mackerel (see page 20)*

Broad bean quinoa

Quinoa is a high-protein carbohydrate and wonderful as an alternative to rice; in fact, this is cooked in a similar way, and is almost like a broad bean pulao. Always check if the grain is properly cooked before serving, then, if there's any liquid remaining in the pan, just drain it off. This is just one way of using quinoa with an Indian accent; it's also great in a salad with tomatoes, feta and red onions.

100g quinoa
salt
2 tbsp vegetable oil
1 dried red chilli, broken into 2–3 pieces
1 tsp black mustard seeds
2–3 sprigs of fresh curry leaves
1 large onion, finely chopped
1 green chilli, finely chopped
1cm piece of root ginger, finely chopped
1 tomato, finely chopped
¼ tsp chilli powder
100g broad beans, shelled (if frozen, soak in hot water for 10 minutes and remove skins)
1 tsp caster sugar
1 tbsp chopped coriander leaves
1 tbsp chopped basil leaves
1 tbsp chopped chives
juice of ½ lemon or lime

Soak the quinoa in cold water for 15 minutes, then drain and rinse. Put 300ml of water into a saucepan and add the drained quinoa with some salt. Bring to the boil, reduce the heat, then simmer for about 15 minutes, until the grains are cooked but still retain a little bite. Drain off any excess water.

Meanwhile, heat the oil in a heavy-based pan over a medium heat and add the dried chilli and mustard seeds. Allow them to pop and crackle for a few seconds, then add the curry leaves and onion. Cook until it just begins to turn golden. Now add the green chilli and ginger. Stir-fry for a minute, then add the tomato and chilli powder. Continue to cook for a further five minutes or so, until most of the moisture from the tomato has evaporated, then add the broad beans and continue to stir-fry for a few minutes. Now add the cooked quinoa and mix thoroughly for a minute or two until heated through.

Finally, stir in the sugar, herbs and lemon juice. Mix thoroughly, adjust the seasoning and serve.

SERVES 3–4 AS A SIDE DISH

Serve with Tandoori Lamb Racks (*see pag 104*), *or* Beef Tikkas (*see page 100*), *or* Tandoori King Prawn (*see page 87*)

Perfect rice

If you have a tried and tested recipe for making perfect rice, stick to it. This is just how I cook it. The quantities here are enough for four people to go with a meal as an accompaniment. Asian people tend to eat more rice, treating it as the core of a dish and using the curries and side dishes simply as seasonings.

350g basmati rice
salt

Wash the rice in hot water, then rinse in a few changes of cold water until the water runs clear. Soak for 20–30 minutes in salted water. Rinse again to remove the salt, then drain.

Put the drained rice into a saucepan with a tight-fitting lid, adding 450ml of water and 1 tsp salt. Bring to the boil over a medium-high heat and boil until craters begin to show on the surface of the rice. Reduce the heat to a minimum and cover the pan with a clean dry tea towel. Cover with the saucepan lid, and fold back the overhang of the cloth over the lid.

Allow to cook for 15–20 minutes on a low heat. Do not open the lid until at least 15 minutes have passed. Lift the lid and fold with a fork to fluff up the rice.

Coconut rice

Wonderful with anything, and especially flattering to any dish that already contains coconut. It also tames heat, so try it with the Braised and Fried Beef (see page 46) or Laal Maas (see page 108). For a photo, see page 94.

500g basmati rice
salt
1 tbsp ghee or vegetable oil
250ml coconut milk
2 tbsp toasted desiccated coconut

TO SERVE
2 tbsp fried onions

Wash the rice in hot water, then rinse it several times in cold water to remove as much starch as possible. Leave to soak in salted water for 15 minutes. Drain and wash the rice again to remove the salt.

In a heavy-based pan with a tight-fitting lid, heat the ghee or oil over a medium heat, add the rice and gently sauté until the grains are coated with the oil. Add 800ml of water, salt, and the coconut milk. Bring to the boil. Cook the rice until most of the liquid has been absorbed and small craters appear on the surface.

Place a clean dry tea towel over the saucepan and cover with the lid. Leave to simmer on a very low heat for 15–20 minutes. Do not lift the lid during this time. Remove from the heat. Lift the lid and gently fold in the coconut. Serve on a platter, scattered with the fried onions.

SERVES 4–6

Spinach and leek rice

This is a fabulous rice dish, and one I turn to again and again. I hope that soon you'll do the same. It is pure green and the flavours of the dill and fenugreek are simply heaven. For a photo, see page 102.

2 tsp cumin seeds
450g basmati rice
800g spinach, washed, dried, and chopped
4–5 tbsp vegetable oil
225g leeks, washed, dried, and chopped
1 tbsp dried dill
1 tsp ground fenugreek seeds
salt
freshly ground black pepper

Put the cumin seeds in a small dry frying pan and place over a medium heat. Stir until they turn a shade darker and smell aromatic. Set aside.

Rinse the rice in several changes of water until the water runs clear. Leave to soak in fresh water for about 30 minutes.

Preheat the oven to 150°C/300°F/gas mark 2.

Put the spinach into a large pan and add 150ml water and 2–3 tbsp of the oil. Place on a medium-high heat and boil for five minutes, stirring occasionally, until the spinach wilts and the water becomes green. Drain off the water and oil from the spinach into a bowl, reserving the liquid.

Heat the remaining oil in a separate pan and add the leeks. Cook over a medium heat until soft, but not brown. Add this to the spinach with the dill, fenugreek, salt and pepper. Add a little of the reserved spinach liquid, retaining 125ml for the rice. Cook until all the liquid evaporates and the spinach is soft.

Bring 1.5 litres of water to the boil with 1 tsp salt. Drain the rice and add to the boiling water. Par-boil for three to four minutes, then drain into a colander. Put the rice into a pot with a tight-fitting lid and add the spinach and leek mixture with the cumin. Adjust the seasoning with black pepper. Now add the reserved 125ml spinach water. Fold gently into the spinach and leeks. Cover the pot with the lid and bake in the oven for 30–45 minutes. Alternatively, cook over a low heat on the hob for 20–25 minutes.

SERVES 6

Saffron rice

I often use a tea towel, as here, to help seal the saucepan when cooking rice. The fabric absorbs all the moisture, keeping the rice light and fluffy.

400g basmati rice
½ tsp saffron threads
a little whole milk, warmed
2 tbsp ghee or vegetable oil
4–5 cardamom pods
3 cloves
2 x 2.5cm cinnamon sticks
salt

Rinse the rice in warm water, then rinse in a few changes of cold water until the water runs clear, removing as much starch as possible. Now soak the rice for about 20 minutes, drain in a colander and leave to dry for another 10 minutes.

Meanwhile, soak the saffron in a little warm milk for 10 minutes.

Heat the ghee or oil over a medium-high heat in a heavy-based saucepan which has a tight-fitting lid. Add the cardamom pods, cloves and cinnamon, allow them to crackle for a few seconds, then add the drained rice and stir to coat the grains. Add the saffron mixture, 700ml of water and some salt. Bring to the boil, stir once, then cook until most of the liquid has evaporated and small craters form on the surface. Reduce the heat to a minimum. Place a clean, dry tea towel over the mouth of the saucepan and cover tightly with a lid, wrapping the towel over the lid.

Leave the rice on the heat for about 15 minutes. Take off the lid and gently fork through, lifting, loosening and fluffing up the rice. Have a quick taste to check it's done. If it still has a little way to go, replace the lid and continue to cook for three minutes. Remove from the heat and allow to rest for a few minutes, then serve.

SERVES 4–6

Jewelled rice

I know this is a long-winded dish, but it is a rice of all rices. Serve it on festive occasions. Barberries are widely available in Middle Eastern stores but, if they are hard to find, use dried cranberries. For a photo, see page 69.

FOR THE SPICE MIX
2 tbsp dried rose petals, ground
2 tbsp ground cardamom
2 tbsp ground cinnamon
1 tbsp fennel seeds, ground

FOR THE RICE
400g basmati rice
salt
finely grated zest of 3 oranges
and juice of 1
2 large carrots, cut into julienne
2.5cm piece of root
ginger, grated
100g caster sugar
4 onions, thinly sliced
4–6 tbsp rapeseed oil or ghee,
plus more for layering the rice
2–3 garlic cloves, crushed
4 tbsp barberries, washed and
drained thoroughly (optional)
4 tbsp dried cherries
4 tbsp raisins
1 tsp saffron threads soaked
with 4 tbsp hot milk
for 15 minutes
240ml chicken stock
4 tbsp slivered pistachios

Combine all the spices for the spice mix together and store in an airtight container. You will need about 2 tsp for this recipe. Preheat the oven to 200°C/400°F/gas mark 6.

Wash the rice in hot water, then rinse several times in cold water to remove as much starch as possible. Soak in cold water with salt for at least 30 minutes. Rinse and drain.

In the meantime, put the orange zest into a saucepan and cover with water. Bring to the boil and drain. Return the zest to the pan with the carrots, ginger, sugar and 240ml water. Bring to the boil and boil for eight to 10 minutes. Drain and set aside.

Fry the onions in the oil or ghee over a medium-high heat until golden brown, then add the garlic. Now add the barberries (if using), dried cherries and raisins. Cook for a minute. Remove and set aside. (Reserve one-third of the mixture for serving.)

Using a separate large saucepan – one which has a tight-fitting lid – bring 1.5 litres of water to the boil. Once the water reaches a rolling boil, add the drained rice with some salt and a drizzle of ghee or oil to keep the grains separate. Boil briskly for one to two minutes to par-cook, then strain through a colander. Immediately run cold water over the rice to stop the cooking process, then leave to stand.

Using the same pan, melt 4 tbsp ghee or oil and cover the base with a layer of the par-cooked rice. Drizzle with a small amount of the saffron milk and a pinch of the spice mix. Now place two spatulas of rice on top with some of the carrot mixture, ½ tsp of spice mix, a sprinkling of saffron milk and some of the fried onion mixture. Repeat until you have used all the rice, carrot and onion mixtures.

Mix the orange juice with the stock and pour over the rice. Drizzle over any leftover saffron milk. Cover the pan with a clean tea towel and the lid. Place in the oven for 10 minutes, then reduce the oven temperature to 180°C/350°F/gas mark 4 and cook for 20 minutes. Remove from the oven and serve the rice on a large platter with the pistachio nuts and reserved fried onion mixture.

SERVES 6

Chutneys, raitas and relishes

In India, no meal is complete without bowls of delightful relishes, which sparkle on the palate. For humble meals, these are enough to season a whole plate of rice, without any other accompaniment. Served with a whole meal, they really take it over the edge. Each one of these is a fabulous recipe to have in your repertoire.

Shredded green mango pickle

FOR THE PICKLE
1 tsp cumin seeds
2 tsp coriander seeds
6 medium-sized green unripe mangoes
2 tsp chilli powder
¼ tsp turmeric
1 tsp ground mustard seeds
80ml cider vinegar
4-5 tbsp caster sugar
salt

FOR THE TEMPERING
150-160ml vegetable oil
1 tsp black mustard seeds
2 tsp cumin seeds
½ tsp nigella seeds
½ tsp fenugreek seeds

Put the cumin and coriander seeds into a small dry frying pan and place over a medium heat. Stir until the seeds have darkened slightly and smell aromatic. Tip into a mortar and grind to a powder with the pestle. Wash and dry the mangoes and peel them. Grate the flesh, discarding the stone. Place the grated mangoes into a mixing bowl and add all the other ingredients for the pickle.

Heat the oil in a frying pan until hot over a medium-high flame. Once the oil begins to smoke, add the mustard and cumin seeds. Once they pop and splutter, add the nigella and the fenugreek seeds. After a few seconds, remove from the heat and allow to cool. Once cool, pour on to the grated mango. Transfer into a clean, dry airtight jar.
SERVES 6–8

Smoked aubergine raita with sesame seeds

1 large, plump aubergine
1 tsp cumin seeds
2 tbsp olive oil
juice of 1 lemon
2 garlic cloves, crushed
200g Greek yogurt, lightly whisked
1 tbsp toasted sesame seeds
3 spring onions, finely chopped
1 tbsp finely chopped mint
salt
freshly ground black pepper

Put the aubergines directly on the gas flame on top of the stove or under a grill, turning them from time to time until the skin is charred on all sides and the flesh feels soft. Meanwhile, put the cumin seeds in a dry frying pan and stir over a medium heat until slightly darker and aromatic. Tip into a mortar and grind coarsely with the pestle. Put the aubergine either into a plastic bag or a bowl covered with cling film. Leave for 10 minutes or so. This will help the skin to come off easily. Hold the aubergine by the stalk under cold running water and gently peel off the charred skin until you are left with just the smooth bulbous flesh. Squeeze the flesh with your fingers to get rid of any excess water and place on to a chopping board. Chop to a pulp, discarding the stalk.

Put the aubergine flesh into a bowl with the olive oil, lemon juice and garlic. Beat well to mix, then fold in the yogurt, sesame seeds, cumin, spring onions and mint. Season to taste and serve either chilled or at room temperature. **SERVES 6–8**

Cucumber raita

1½ tsp cumin seeds
1 cucumber, grated
350ml Greek yogurt
¼ bunch mint, leaves picked and
finely chopped
½ lemon, juiced
salt

Put the cumin seeds into a small dry frying pan, place over a medium heat and stir until the seeds are slightly darker and smell aromatic. Tip into a mortar and grind to a powder with the pestle.

Once the cucumber has been grated, squeeze it to remove as much liquid as possible. Place into a bowl and add the remaining ingredients. Season with salt to taste, mix well and serve immediately. **SERVES 6–8**

Coriander and walnut chutney

1 bunch fresh coriander leaves,
roughly chopped
10-12 hot green chillies, deseeded
2-3 garlic cloves, peeled
25g walnuts
25g raisins
25g caster sugar
juice of 4 lemons
2 tsp salt

Put the coriander, green chillies, garlic, walnuts and raisins into the bowl of a food processor and pulse a few times. Make sure it does not turn into a paste. Add the sugar and lemon juice and pulse once more to combine. Add salt to taste. It's now ready to serve, but can be kept in an airtight container in the fridge for up to a week. **SERVES 4–6**

Sambal with lemon grass

75g tamarind pulp
150g red chillies
130g shallots, roughly chopped
3 garlic cloves
5 tbsp vegetable oil
1 lemon grass stalk, outer skin peeled
and lightly smashed
50g caster sugar
salt

Soak the tamarind pulp in 150ml of hot water for 30 minutes, then strain, pushing the pulp through a sieve to extract the maximum amount. Blend together the chillies, shallots, garlic, 1 tbsp of the oil and approximately 150ml water into a food processor, blitzing to a fairly thick, smooth paste. Heat the remaining oil in a frying pan over a medium heat until hot, then add the paste and the lemon grass. Sauté the paste until the oil begins to rise to the surface, then add the sugar and salt. Keep cooking until the oil separates again, then add the tamarind. Continue to stir-fry until the mixture glistens and has an almost jam-like consistency. Allow to cool, then discard the lemon grass. **SERVES 8**

Coriander and yogurt dip

80 coriander leaves and stalks,
roughly chopped
3 garlic cloves
4 green chillies
juice of 2 limes and finely grated zest of 1
3-4 tsp caster sugar
2-3 tbsp yogurt
salt, to taste

Put all the ingredients in a food processor or blender and blitz until smooth and runny. Place into a bowl and adjust the seasoning. Refrigerate until required. **SERVES 4**

Sweet *like* CANDY

White chocolate, cardamom and rose pannacotta

This is such a lovely dish. If you can melt chocolate, you can make this impressive and delicious pudding, as the gelatine does all the hard work for you. Any sort of chocolate works fabulously with cardamom. Rose syrup can be very sweet on its own but, cut with lime juice as it is here, it makes the perfect, fragrant accompaniment. If you can't find rose syrup, make a simple sugar syrup and flavour to taste with rose water. Together, the pannacotta and syrup form a wonderful balance of sweet, sharp and aromatic. Use any berries in season; all should work well.

FOR THE PANNACOTTA
200g good-quality white chocolate, such as Valrhona
400ml whipping cream
200ml whole milk
75g caster sugar
1 tsp ground cardamom seeds
3 gelatine leaves

FOR THE ROSE SYRUP
6 tbsp rose syrup
½ tsp ground cardamom seeds
finely grated zest and juice of 1 lime

TO SERVE
24 strawberries, hulled and halved, or quartered if large
24 raspberries
6 sprigs of redcurrants
1–2 tbsp slivered pistachios

Melt the chocolate with the cream, milk and sugar in a heatproof bowl suspended over a saucepan of gently simmering water. Make sure the base of the bowl does not touch the water. Once melted, whisk until the sugar dissolves, then stir in the cardamom.

Meanwhile, soak the gelatine leaves in cold water for five minutes, until soft and pliable. Squeeze out excess water and add to the chocolate mixture. Stir until the gelatine has dissolved. Strain the mixture through a fine sieve and pour into six moulds, each about 150ml in capacity. Allow to cool, then refrigerate for at least four hours, until set.

Put all the ingredients for the rose syrup into a pan with 2 tbsp water. Bring to the boil, then remove from the heat and set aside to infuse for 30 minutes. Strain through a fine sieve.

Turn out the pannacottas; this is easier if you first dip the moulds into very hot water. Place one pannacotta in the centre of each of six plates. Spoon around the rose syrup. Arrange the berries and currants around and sprinkle with the pistachios.

SERVES 6

Vermicelli pudding

This was originally a royal pudding. It's a wonderfully rich, sweet celebratory dish, made in Muslim homes all over the subcontinent, traditionally during the festival of Eid, but also for weddings and other parties. I realise a pudding made from fine angel's hair pasta might be a new one on you, but you should try this. The lemon juice gives a slight sharpness which stops it from being too cloying. It is best to use the very fine, delicate Indian pasta known as *seviyan*, which you'll find in any Indian food shop, but you can also use the thicker Italian vermicelli. To cook this dish, it's best to use a wok, because it allows the moisture to evaporate much more efficiently than a saucepan.

350g caster sugar
4 tbsp ghee
200g vermicelli, ideally seviyan, broken into 15cm lengths
10–12 roughly ground green cardamom pods
500–600ml whole milk
squeeze of lemon juice
generous pinch of saffron threads
1–2 tbsp flaked almonds
1–2 tbsp slivered pistachios
1 tbsp rose water

Put the sugar in a pan with 400ml of water and bring to the boil. Remove from the heat and set aside.

Melt the ghee over a low heat in a wok or wide saucepan. Add the vermicelli and crushed cardamom. Fry over a medium-high heat, stirring the vermicelli around so they brown evenly. Once the vermicelli have turned a light golden brown, pour in the sugar syrup and continue to cook over a low heat for about 15 minutes. It will bubble furiously as the water evaporates. Stir occasionally to ensure the vermicelli do not stick to the pan. As the water evaporates, the vermicelli will stiffen a little and the ghee will separate.

At this stage, add the milk. Bring to the boil, then add the lemon juice. The liquid will instantly be reabsorbed by the vermicelli. Continue to stir-fry for a few minutes, then add the saffron, almonds, pistachios and rose water. Continue to fry for a minute or so. Serve hot or cold, but this is best served 20 minutes after cooking.

SERVES 4–6

Turinois

This is a classic dish that I have resurrected from the 1960s. It is a very dense chocolate and chestnut terrine. When you add water to chocolate and melt it, the chocolate hardens when it sets, so that's why it's in here. Well worth doing, the turinois takes only 15 minutes prep, then the fridge does all the work. I sometimes add cinnamon and nutmeg, but here I've simply used cardamom. All those spices are fabulous in combination with chestnuts. For those who like a tipple, if you fancy adding a glug of brandy, do so!

3 x 240g cans vacuum-packed chestnuts
140g unsalted butter
140g caster sugar
½ tsp vanilla extract
240g good-quality dark chocolate
1 tsp ground cardamom seeds
vegetable oil, for the tin
3–4 marrons glacés, crumbled

Put all the vacuum-packed chestnuts into a food processor and grind to a fine powder. Set aside.

Cream the butter thoroughly in a bowl with an electric whisk. Add the sugar gradually until the mixture is light and fluffy. Add the vanilla.

Break up the chocolate and place in a heavy-based pan. Pour in 150ml of water and the cardamom and melt over a very low heat. Allow to cool a little, then pour into the butter mixture. Add the ground chestnuts and mix thoroughly.

Lightly oil a 900g loaf tin, then line with cling film, making sure there are no air gaps or bubbles. Pour in the chocolate mixture and knock the tin on a flat surface to remove any air bubbles.

Cover with cling film and refrigerate for eight hours, or overnight. Turn out on to a plate and arrange the marrons glacés on top. Cut into thin slices and serve with crème fraîche.

SERVES 8–10

Mango brûlée

A simple sweet with exotic ingredients. Just make sure that, when you take it from the oven, it still has a wobble in the middle, as it will continue to cook after it comes out of the oven and you need to keep it tender, not rubbery.

325ml double cream
50g caster sugar
200ml canned mango purée
½ tsp ground cardamom seeds
1 egg, plus 3 egg yolks
100g demerara sugar

Preheat the oven to 150°C/300°F/gas mark 2.

Put the cream, caster sugar, mango purée and cardamom into a pan and bring to a simmering point, stirring occasionally. Whisk the egg and egg yolks together in a bowl and slowly pour in the mango mixture, whisking continuously.

Pour the mixture into six ramekins, each of about 150ml capacity, and place in a roasting tin. Pull out the oven shelf, rest the roasting tin on it, and pour in hot water from the kettle to come halfway up the sides of the ramekins. Bake for 20–25 minutes, or until just set. Start checking after 15 minutes, in case your oven is running hot; there should be a wobble in the middle when you take the brulées from the oven.

Remove the ramekins from the roasting tin and leave to cool, before putting into the fridge to chill.

Sprinkle the demerara sugar evenly on top of each brûlée, then place the ramekins under a very hot grill until the sugar has caramelised. Chill once more before serving.

SERVES 6

Poached pears with saffron, cinnamon and star anise

These wonderful pears can be made a day in advance and kept, chilled, in the fridge; this will intensify the colour and flavour. If the pears are very hard it will take a little longer to poach them until they are tender all the way through. You may find they need up to an hour, because some of the hardest pears seem to take forever! Very ripe pears won't need much time at all. I like to use Comice pears for this pudding, if possible. Serve them with crème fraîche, mascarpone cheese or thick Greek yogurt. Served standing up, these are pears on parade!

6 small, equal-sized pears
150g caster sugar
3 star anise
1 cinnamon stick, or 2 cassia barks
generous pinch of saffron threads
finely grated zest of 1 unwaxed lemon and juice of ½

Peel the pears, leaving the stalks intact. Cut a very thin slice from the base of each pear so that it sits upright. Place in a bowl of water to prevent them from discolouring.

In the meantime, put the sugar, 1 litre of water, the star anise, cinnamon or cassia, saffron and lemon zest in a saucepan big enough to hold the pears. Heat gently until the sugar dissolves, then bring to the boil. Add the pears, reduce the heat and poach at a gentle simmer for up to one hour, until tender to the point of a knife.

Remove the pears from the poaching liquid and lie them flat in a deep dish which will hold both the pears and the syrup.

Return the poaching liquid to the boil, and bubble for 10 minutes or so until the liquid is well reduced and syrupy. Squeeze over the lemon juice and strain the syrup evenly over the pears. When ready to serve, stand the pears upright and spoon over the syrup.

SERVES 6

Rose petal and cardamom kulfi

A traditional Indian ice cream that does not contain any eggs. Because of this, it is best to take your kulfi from the freezer and put it into the fridge for about 10 minutes before serving, to soften slightly. For a kulfi, milk is thickened and cooked so most of the water content is driven off and it becomes very rich and thick. To eat this as a popsicle, as in the photo, stick a lolly stick in the kulfi while it is freezing but before it has fully hardened. Immerse the moulds or ramekins in hot water to turn out the kulfi, then roll them in a bowl of crushed pistachios. Cooling kulfi, a perfect lick on a stick!

600ml whole milk
300ml double cream
100ml rose syrup
½ tsp ground cardamom
petals from 2 unsprayed red roses, washed, finely chopped
2 tbsp finely chopped pistachios

Bring the milk and cream to the boil in a heavy-based saucepan. Reduce the heat and simmer, stirring continuously, until the mixture has reduced to one-third of its original volume. Allow to cool.

Add the rose syrup, cardamom and rose petals to the reduced milk. Allow to cool before putting in the fridge for three hours.

Churn the chilled milk mixture in an ice cream machine until it begins to set. Scoop into either dariole moulds or ramekin dishes. Freeze for three to four hours, or until well set. Soften the kulfi (see recipe introduction) and sprinkle over the pistachios to serve.

SERVES 6

Roasted rhubarb and almond tartlets

Cardamom is lovely in combination with rhubarb, its sweet fragrance flattering the astringency of the stalks. This makes a lovely light dessert, so unlike Indian sweets, which can be heavy and cloying. This recipe uses Indian ingredients – almonds, oranges and sugar – with rhubarb, which is a very English fruit (actually, vegetable). In season, these are lovely served with berries; raspberries are especially good, as are strawberries.

FOR THE TARTLETS
450g rhubarb, trimmed
250g caster sugar
½ tsp ground cardamom
finely grated zest and juice of
1 large orange
320g ready-rolled puff pastry
1 egg, beaten
2–3 tbsp toasted hazelnuts
or almonds
icing sugar, to dust

FOR THE ALMOND PASTE
100g ground almonds
60g caster sugar
3 tbsp thick double cream

Preheat the oven to 150°C/300°F/gas mark 2. Spread the rhubarb out in a single layer in a large roasting tin. Sprinkle over the sugar, cardamom and orange zest. Pour over the juice.

Cover the tin with foil and roast for up to an hour, until tender. Strain out the juice and pour into a saucepan. Bring the juice to the boil, rduce the heat and simmer until it has thickened and reduced by half. Allow to cool.

Meanwhile, mix together the ground almonds, sugar and cream to a smooth paste in a mixing bowl and set aside. Increase the oven temperature to 180°C/350°F/gas mark 4.

Cut the puff pastry into six equal-sized squares. Place on a large baking tray lined with baking parchment. Using a sharp knife, create a rim on each square by scoring a line about 1cm away from each edge, without cutting through the pastry. Spread the almond paste over the pastry, not covering the rim. Brush the rim with beaten egg and place in the oven. Bake for 10–12 minutes.

Cut the rhubarb into strips and place on the tarts. Drizzle with some of the rhubarb syrup and sprinkle with the toasted nuts. Dust with icing sugar. Serve the rest of the syrup on the side with a generous dollop of clotted cream.

SERVES 6

Rice pudding with rose petal jam

This is very rich, intense and decadent and perhaps not for the calorie conscious. Throw away all your cholesterol worries and eat it. A very traditional Indian dessert, this makes a good hot pud for a winter's day. Rose petal jam, which you can buy in Middle Eastern shops, gives you that lovely feeling of eating Turkish delight. Truly a pudding of eastern promise...

250g short-grain pudding rice
600ml double cream
800ml whole milk
120g caster sugar
½ tsp ground cardamom
3 tbsp rose water
juice of 1 lime
3–4 tbsp rose petal jam
50g pistachios, chopped
2 tbsp dried rose petals

Preheat the oven to 180°C/350°F/gas mark 4.

Wash and drain the rice and put into a heavy-based saucepan. Add half the cream and cook over a medium heat for a few minutes, then add all the milk, sugar and cardamom. Cook over a low heat for 20–30 minutes, stirring regularly, until the rice grains become soft and the liquid has more or less been absorbed. Remove from the heat. Whip the remaining double cream to soft peaks and fold into the rice pudding. Mix gently. Finish by stirring through the rose water and lime juice.

In a separate saucepan, gently warm the rose petal jam with a dash of water until loose and runny. Remove from the heat and set aside.

Pour the rice pudding into individual dishes. Add 1 tbsp of the runny rose petal jam to each. Sprinkle with the pistachios and rose petals.

SERVES 6–8

Beetroot samosas

We always expect samosas to be savoury. In this unusual recipe, a sugared sweetness breaks through the earthiness of the beetroot, while the ricotta cheese gives a lovely richness. Make sure you don't use beetroot in vinegar… that would be a bit of a disaster! This is a wonderful way to convince beetroot naysayers to think again.

FOR THE SAMOSAS
250g cooked beetroot
½ tsp ground cardamom
25g raisins
30g coconut, finely grated
3–4 tbsp caster sugar
30g ricotta cheese, crumbled
125g unsalted butter
250g filo pastry
2 tbsp black poppy seeds
2 tbsp white sesame seeds
icing sugar, to dust

FOR THE LIME DIP
120g jaggery, or 110g soft dark brown sugar
finely grated zest and juice of ½ lime

Finely grate the beetroot and strain off any of the juices. Heat a frying pan and put in the grated beetroot with half the cardamom. Cook just until no moisture remains in the beetroot. Add the raisins, coconut and sugar and continue to cook for a few more minutes. Remove from the heat and allow to cool in a bowl. Now crumble in the ricotta and add the remaining cardamom. Mix well and set aside.

Preheat the oven to 200°C/400°F/gas mark 6. Melt the butter. Lay a sheet of filo pastry on a work surface and brush with melted butter. Place a second sheet on top to fit exactly over the first, then cut the filo pastry into strips about 5cm wide. Spoon a heaped teaspoon of filling into one corner of the strip. Fold the right corner of the strip over to the left side to create a triangle. Continue to fold the triangle along the strip until you reach the end, and cut off any surplus pastry. Repeat until you have used up all the pastry and filling.

Brush the samosas liberally with butter and sprinkle with poppy and sesame seeds. Bake in the hot oven for 10–12 minutes, until the pastry is cooked and golden.

For the dip, put the jaggery or sugar into a saucepan and add 200ml of water. Cook over a low heat, stirring, until the sugar dissolves, then increase the heat and cook until syrupy. Add the lime zest and juice and leave to cool. Drizzle the lime dip over the samosas and dust with icing sugar to serve.

MAKES 12–15

Acknowledgements

To all at Quadrille who have helped in making this book come to life, especially Anne for commissioning me and Katherine for her beautiful design.

To my literary agent Diana, for making it happen. To Warwick, who gave me a kitchen to use while I was so desperate when my own blew up.

To Lucy for helping me with my words, organising my thoughts and keeping me sane.

To Aya for her extraordinary styling talent, Tamzin for her amazing eye, and to Martin Poole for his stunning photography.

To all my friends who have supported me with this project, especially Carolyn, Zelie and Sammy-Jo. And all the rest – they know who they are!

Editorial Director Anne Furniss
Creative Director Helen Lewis
Project Editor Lucy Bannell
Designer Katherine Keeble
Photographer Martin Poole
Prop Stylist Tamzin Ferdinando
Food Stylist Aya Nishimura
Production Director Vincent Smith
Production Controller Leonie Kellman

First published in 2012 by
Quadrille Publishing Limited
Alhambra House
27–31 Charing Cross Road
London WC2H 0LS
www.quadrille.co.uk

Text © 2012 Reza Mahammad
Photography © 2012 Martin Poole
Design and layout © 2012 Quadrille Publishing Ltd

Cataloguing in Publication Data: a catalogue record for this book is available from the British Library.

ISBN 978 1 84949 141 9

Printed in China